5-STRING BASS

Complete Book of Scales, Modes and Chords
by Brian Emmel

T0088536

Cover Photo - Alan Pezzuto
Layout and Production - Ron Middlebrook

SAN 683-8022

ISBN   978-0-931759-61-1

A very special thanks to:
Bass Collection of Meisel Music, GHS strings, Isamu Noguchi's "California Scenario" and Southcoast Plaza Town Center of Costa Mesa CA, Alan Pezzuto and "Picture This Productions", Ava Roberts and "Heartthrob Talent", Chris Baker, Bobby MacNeil, Scott Alexander, Frank Green and "Working Musician", Mark Egan, and to God who brought all these wonderful people together to assist.

CONTENTS

-FOREWORD-

This is one of the best books I've seen for the comprehensive study of Scales, Modes, and Chords for the 5-string bass. This is definately a thesaurus of vital information that will be helpful to all levels of bassists. This book is a must for 4, 5, and 6-string players.

Mark Egan

The Author

Brian Lee Emmel grew up in Northern Ohio where he began playing electric guitar at the age of 14, and later switched to bass guitar at 17. After playing in local top 40 bands he decided to devote his time to songwriting and formed a three piece original act which cut a 45 single that received airplay in Indiana, Michigan, and Ohio.

He has relocated to Los Angeles and has completed an education at the Musician's Institute (B.I.T.) in Hollywood, graduating in the top class.

CHAPTER 1

Scale Terminology

Courtesy of SWR Engineering

PHOTO: Michael Friel

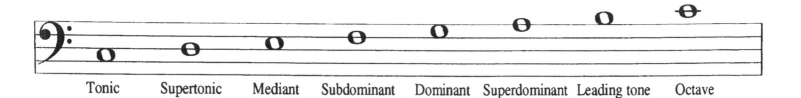

| Tonic | Supertonic | Mediant | Subdominant | Dominant | Superdominant | Leading tone | Octave |

Definition of Scale Degrees

Scales and Modes are constructed from half and whole steps and combinations of the two.

Using C Major or Ionian mode as an example.

1) Tonic: means tone, which in turn indicates the main tone or root tone of the scale.

2) Supertonic: super is a prefix meaning "above". Therefore supertonic indicates the tone above the tone, or the tone above the tonic.

3) Mediant: refers to the third, E, which derives from the tonic triad C-E-G which constructs a C major chord. Mediant means middle or center.

4) Subdominant: means the dominant below the dominant. It's harmonic function is valued a little less than the dominant in major and minor keys.

5) Dominant: because of it's harmonic omnipotence in major and minor keys. It is also known as the key center.

6) Subdominant or super Dominant: Dominant "above" the dominant, the sixth degree also exchanges the major key to it's relative minor key, which introduces a whole new harmonic scale structure. The harmonic minor scale.

7) Leading Tone: the word "leading" implying an impending resolution to the octave.

8) Octave: oct-meaning eight, this is the eighth tone of the scale, same tone as the tonic.

DIATONIC TRIADS IN MAJOR KEYS

The chart below illustrates the harmonized chord construction from all 12 keys. In each key certain chords can be substituted for other related chords.

Here are the substitution rules:

The 1 chord subs for the 3 & 6 chord and vice versa.
The 2 chord subs for the 4 chord.
The 5 chord subs for the 7 chord.

KEY	I	ii	iii	IV	V	vi	vii
C	C Ma.	D mi.	E mi.	F Ma.	G Ma.	A mi.	B dim.
D	D Ma.	E mi.	F# mi.	G Ma.	A Ma.	B mi.	C# dim.
E	E Ma.	F# mi.	G# mi.	A Ma.	B Ma.	C# mi.	D# dim.
F	F Ma.	G mi.	A mi.	Bb Ma.	C Ma.	D mi.	E dim.
G	G Ma.	A mi.	B mi.	C Ma.	D Ma.	E mi.	F# dim.
A	A Ma.	B mi.	C# mi.	D Ma.	E Ma.	F# mi.	G# dim.
B	B Ma.	C# mi.	D# mi.	E Ma.	F# Ma.	G# mi.	A# dim.
Bb	Bb Ma.	C mi.	D mi.	Eb Ma.	F Ma.	G mi.	A dim.
Eb	Eb Ma.	F mi.	G mi.	Ab Ma.	Bb Ma.	C mi.	D dim.
Ab	Ab Ma.	Bb mi.	C mi.	Db Ma.	Eb Ma.	F mi.	G dim.
Db	Db Ma.	Eb mi.	F mi.	Gb Ma.	Ab Ma.	Bb mi.	C dim.
F#	F# Ma.	G mi.	A#mi.	B Ma.	C# Ma.	D# mi.	E# dim.

The examples given in this book are mostly illustrated in the keys of B and C. I've chosen the key of B for two reasons; one, to make life hard for you, and two, because it's the lowest note on the fifth string in open position. Don't fret, I've included the key of C in all examples also, which have no sharps of flats.

The exercises are presented in horizontal or a diagonal form across the fretboard. A vertical form to gain overall fretboard knowledge, and finally a combination of the two.

-CHAPTER 2-

The Scales You Love To Hate

PHOTO: Jay Blakesberg

Spinal Tap - Derek Smalls on Bass

MODES

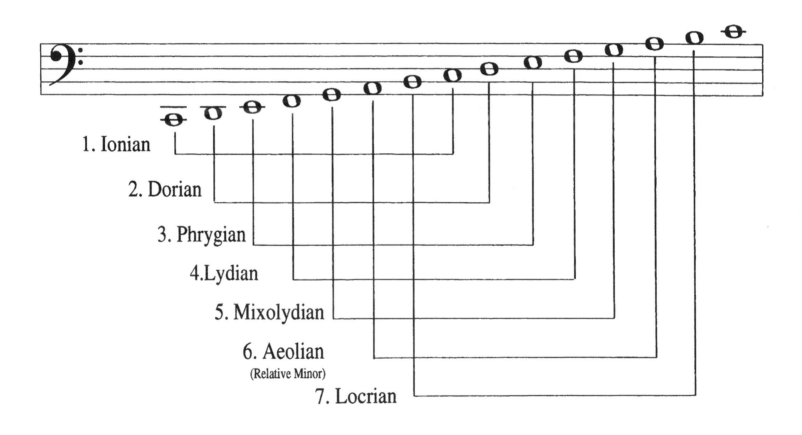

1. Ionian

2. Dorian

3. Phrygian

4. Lydian

5. Mixolydian

6. Aeolian
(Relative Minor)

7. Locrian

Modes

Modes are used to create different harmony affects over a given key, i.e., the key of C major, if using any other than the Ionian mode by starting from any note in the scale and playing up to the same note an octave highter.

Ionian mode plays over:

1) Any major chord unaltered; i.e. Cmajor, Cmajor7, Cmajor6, Cmajor9
   Cmajor6/9, C add9, Cmajor13, Csus4

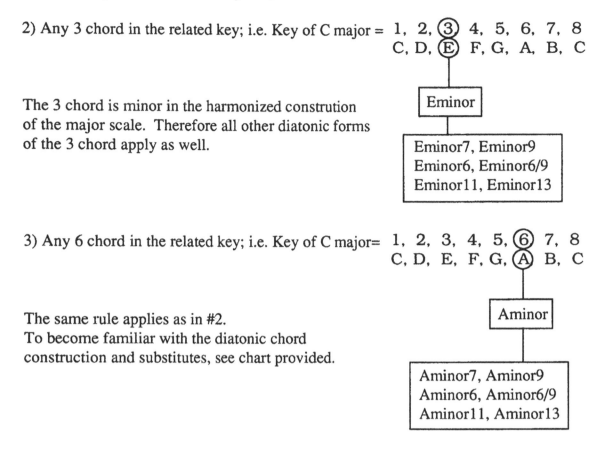

2) Any 3 chord in the related key; i.e. Key of C major = 1, 2, ③ 4, 5, 6, 7, 8
   C, D, Ⓔ F, G, A, B, C

The 3 chord is minor in the harmonized constrution of the major scale. Therefore all other diatonic forms of the 3 chord apply as well.

Eminor

Eminor7, Eminor9
Eminor6, Eminor6/9
Eminor11, Eminor13

3) Any 6 chord in the related key; i.e. Key of C major= 1, 2, 3, 4, 5, ⑥ 7, 8
   C, D, E, F, G, Ⓐ B, C

The same rule applies as in #2.
To become familiar with the diatonic chord construction and substitutes, see chart provided.

Aminor

Aminor7, Aminor9
Aminor6, Aminor6/9
Aminor11, Aminor13

- C Ionian -

Ex.1 Horizontal

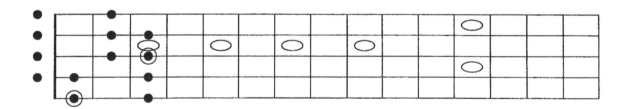

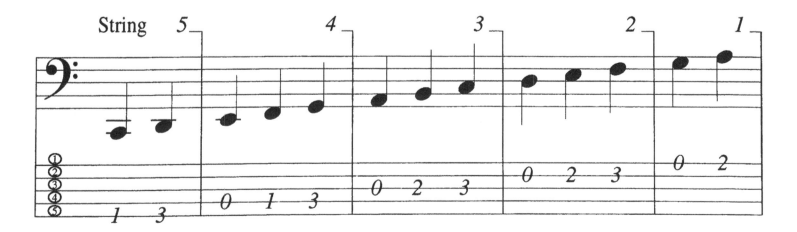

11

Ex. 2 Vertical

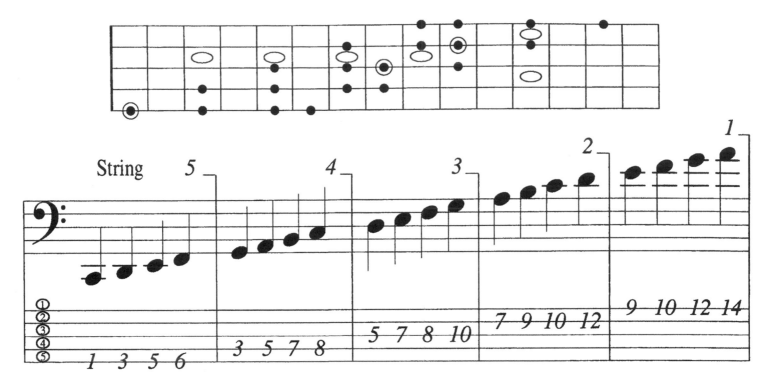

Ex. 3 Horizontal / Vertical

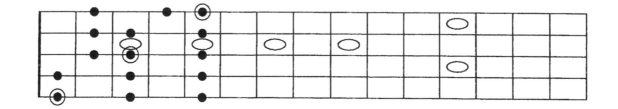

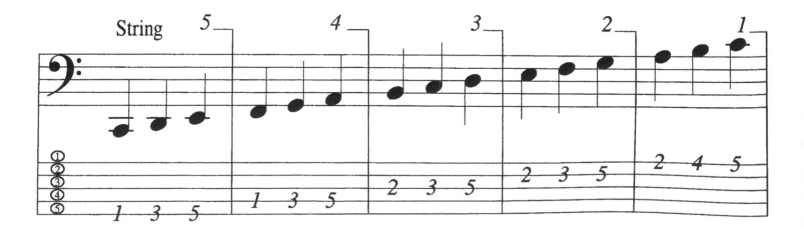

Dorian mode plays over:

1) Any unaltered minor chord or 2 chord in the related key; i.e. Key of C major=

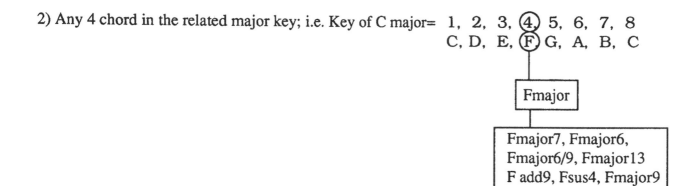

1, ②, 3, 4, 5, 6, 7, 8
C, ⒟ E, F, G, A, B, C

Dminor

Dminor7, Dminor6,
Dminor7sus4, Dminor9
Dminor11, Dminor13

The 2 chord is minor in the harmonized major scale construction.

2) Any 4 chord in the related major key; i.e. Key of C major=

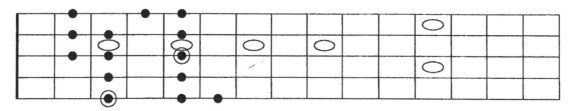

1, 2, 3, ④, 5, 6, 7, 8
C, D, E, Ⓕ G, A, B, C

Fmajor

Fmajor7, Fmajor6,
Fmajor6/9, Fmajor13
F add9, Fsus4, Fmajor9

The 4 chord is major in the harmonized major scale construction.

- D Dorian -

Ex. 1 Horizontal

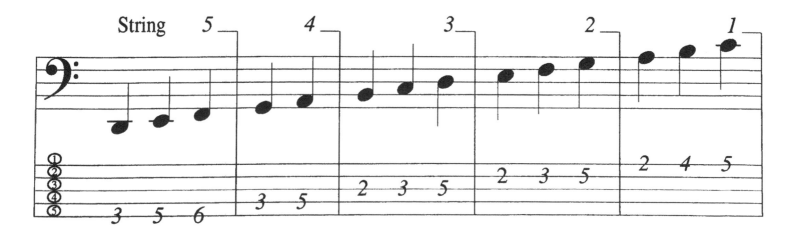

Ex. 2 Vertical

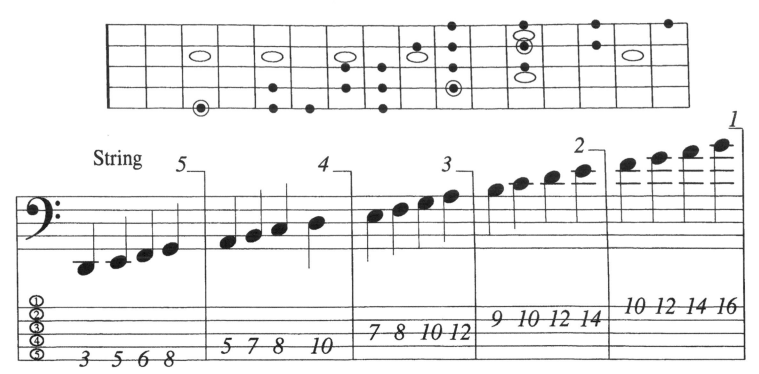

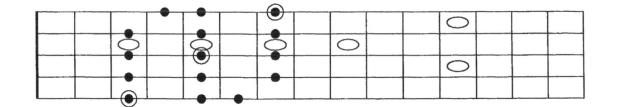

Ex. 3 Horizontal / Vertical

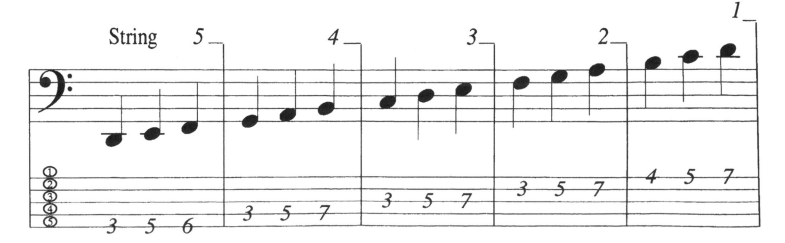

Phrygian mode plays over:

1) Any 3 chord in related major key; i.e. Key of C major= 1, 2, ③ 4, 5, 6, 7, 8
C, D, Ⓔ F, G, A, B, C

The 3 chord is minor in the harmonized construction
of the major scale.

Eminor

Eminor7, Eminor9,
Eminor6, Eminor6/9
Eminor11, Eminor13

2) Any 1 chord in related major key; i.e. Key of C major= ① 2, 3, 4, 5, 6, 7, 8
Ⓒ D, E, F, G, A, B, C

The 1 chord is major in the harmonized construction
of the major scale.

Cmajor

Cmajor7, Cmajor6,
Cmajor9, Cmajor6/9,
Cmajor13, C add9, Csus4

3) Any 6 chord in related major key; i.e. Key of C major= 1, 2, 3, 4, 5, ⑥ 7, 8
C, D, E, F, G, Ⓐ B, C

The 6 chord is minor in the harmonized construction
of the major scale.
The 6th degree is important to remember because it is the
RELATIVE MINOR to it's major key.

Aminor

Aminor7, Aminor6,
Aminor6/9, Aminor9
Aminor7sus4,
Aminor11, Aminor13

Ex.1 Horizontal — E Phrygian -

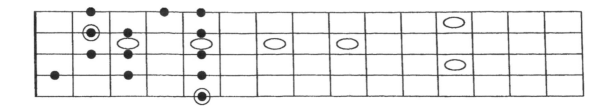

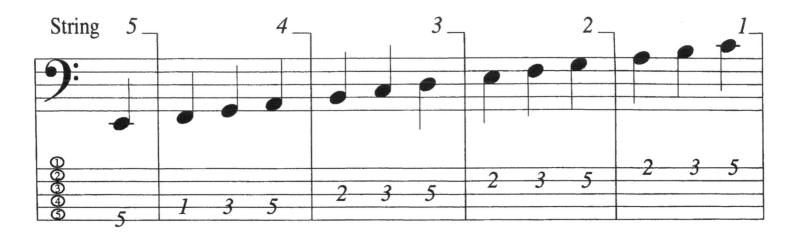

Ex. 2 Vertical

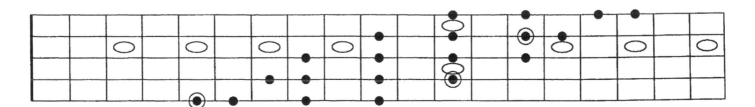

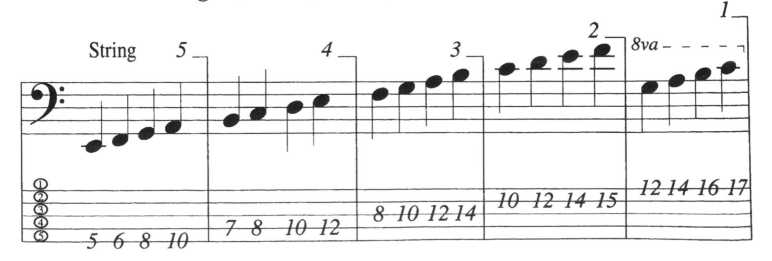

Ex. 3 Horizontal / Vertical

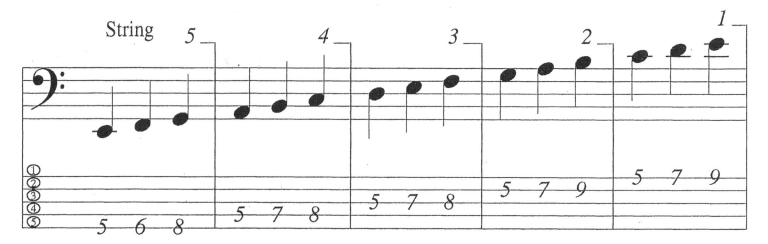

Steve Bailey and Brian Emmel

Lydian mode plays over:

1) Any 4 chord in related key; i.e. Key of C major= 1, 2, 3, ④ 5, 6, 7, 8
   C, D, E, ⓕ G, A, B, C

The 4 chord is major in the harmonized
construction.

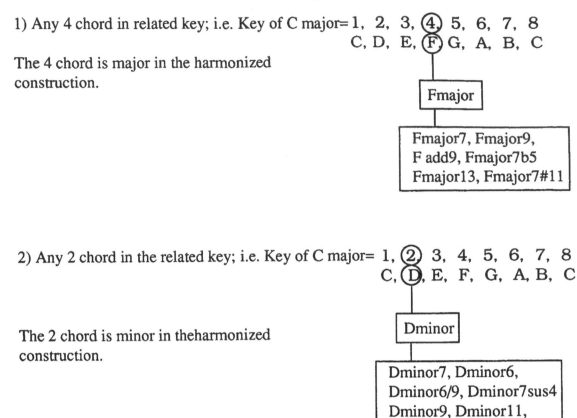

Fmajor

Fmajor7, Fmajor9,
F add9, Fmajor7b5
Fmajor13, Fmajor7#11

2) Any 2 chord in the related key; i.e. Key of C major= 1, ② 3, 4, 5, 6, 7, 8
   C, ⓓ E, F, G, A, B, C

The 2 chord is minor in theharmonized
construction.

Dminor

Dminor7, Dminor6,
Dminor6/9, Dminor7sus4
Dminor9, Dminor11,
Dminor13

- F Lydian -

Ex. 1 Horizontal

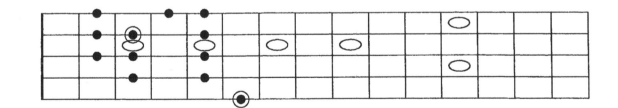

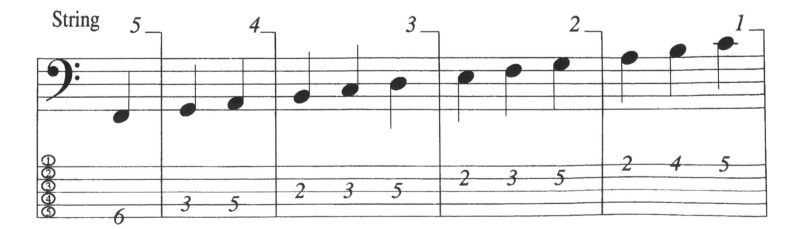

Ex.2 Vertical

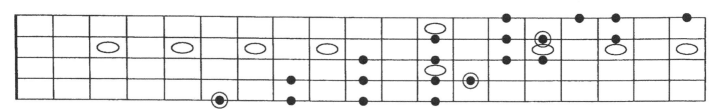

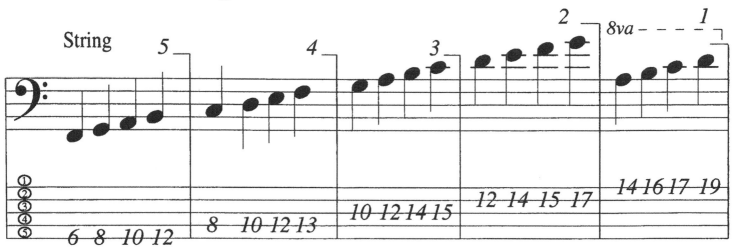

Ex.3 Horizontal / Vertical

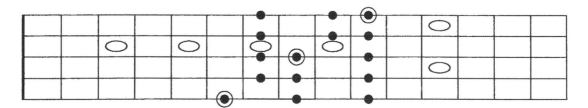

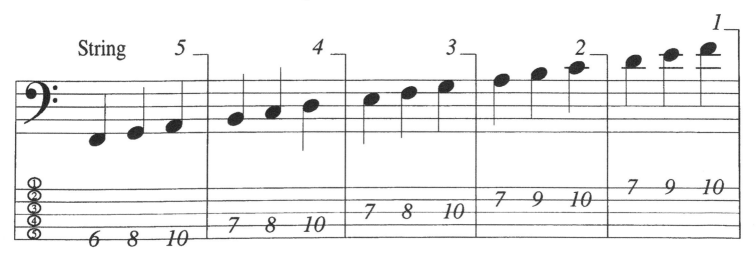

Mixolydian mode plays over:

1) All dominant or 5 chords; i.e. Key of C major = 1, 2, 3, 4, ⑤ 6, 7, 8

C, D, E, F, Ⓖ A, B, C

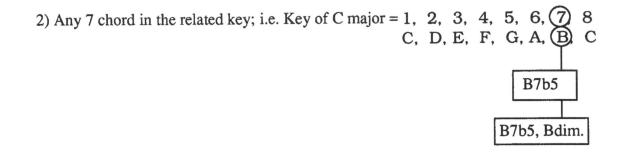

G7

G7, G7sus4, G9, G11, G13

2) Any 7 chord in the related key; i.e. Key of C major = 1, 2, 3, 4, 5, 6, ⑦ 8

C, D, E, F, G, A, Ⓑ C

B7b5

B7b5, Bdim.

Ex.1 Horizontal

- G Mixolydian -

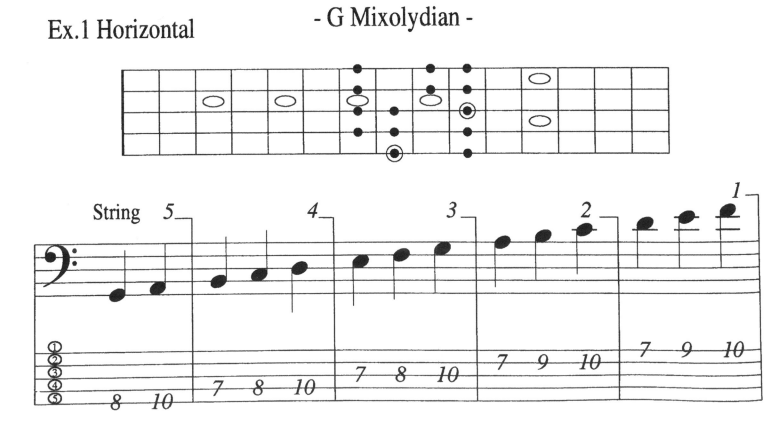

Ex.2 Vertical

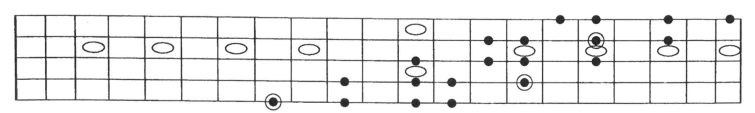

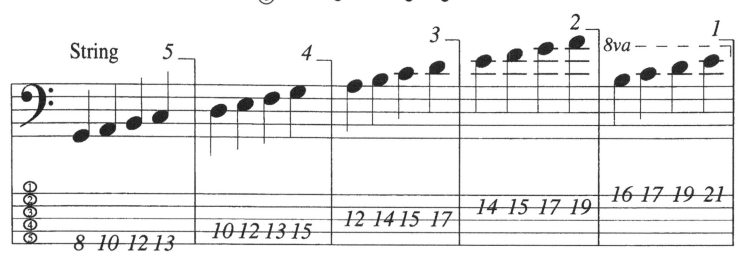

Ex. 3 Horizontal / Vertical

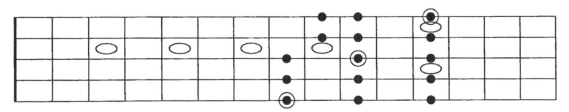

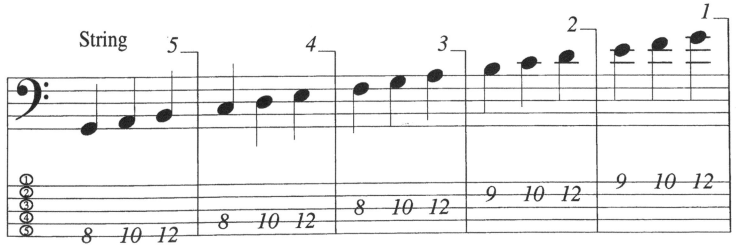

Aeolian mode plays over:

1) Any 6 chord in the related major key; i.e. Key of C major = 1, 2, 3, 4, 5, ⑥ 7, 8
   C, D, E, F, G, Ⓐ B, C

A minor

Aminor7, Aminor9,
Aminor11, Aminor13

2) Any 1 chord in the related major key; i.e. Key of C major = ① 2, 3, 4, 5, 6, 7, 8
   Ⓒ D, E, F, G, A, B, C

Cmajor

Cmajor7, Cmajor6,
Cmajor9, Cmajor6/9
Cadd9, Cmajor13, Csus4

3) The 2 chord of the RELATIVE MINOR key; i.e. Key of C major = Key of A minor

1, 2, 3, 4, 5, ⑥ 7, 8
C, D, E, F, G, Ⓐ B, C

A Harmonic Minor Key

1, ② 3, 4, 5, 6, 7, 8
A, Ⓑ C, D, E, F, G, A

Bminor7b5

22

- A Aeolian -

Ex.1 Horizontal

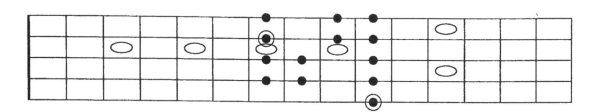

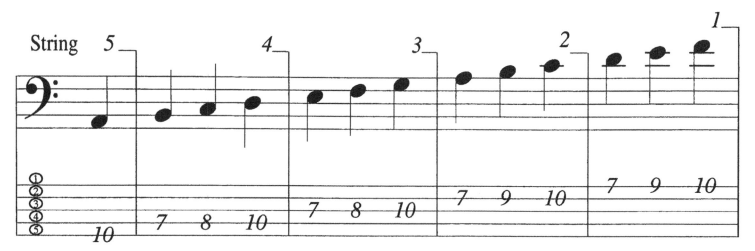

Ex. 2 Vertical

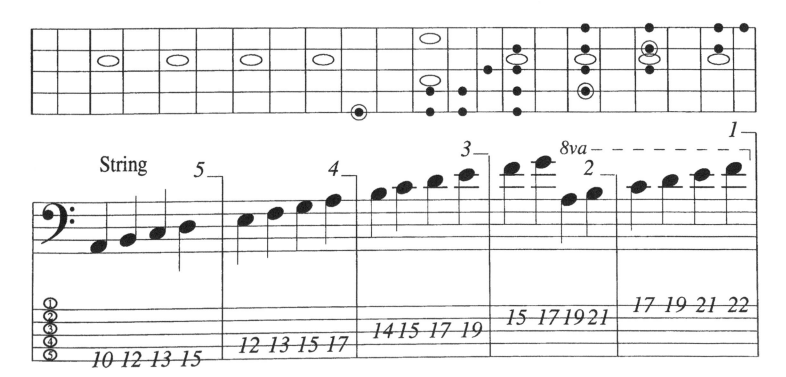

23

Ex.3 Horizontal / Vertical

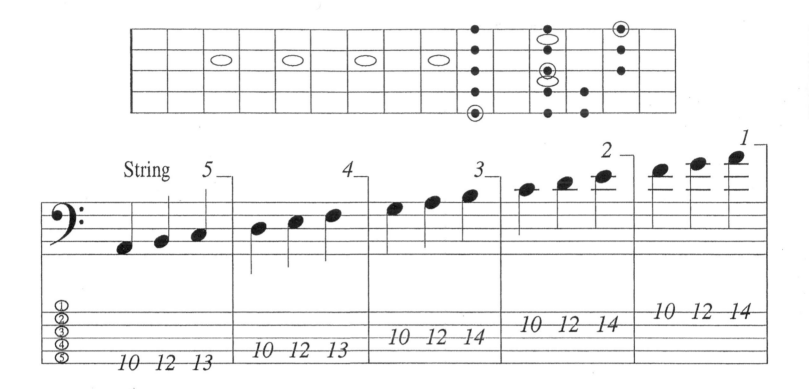

Tune Guitar Technology, Gap 518

<u>Locrian</u> mode plays over:

1) Any 7 chord in the related major key; i.e. Key of C major =

The 7 chord is half diminished or minor in the harmonized construction of the major scale.

2) Any altered dominant chord i.e. C7b5, C7#5, C7b9, C7#9

- B Locrian -

Ex. 1 Horizontal

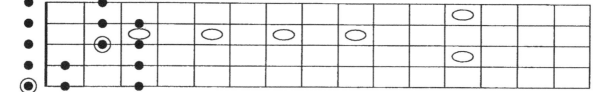

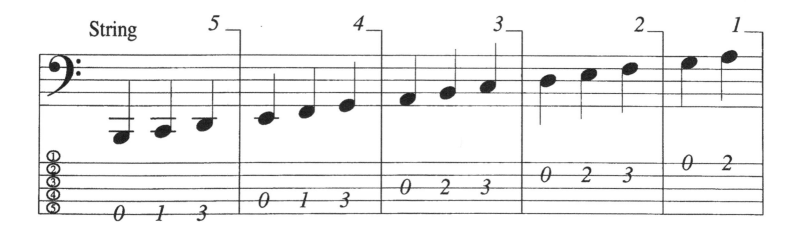

Ex. 2 Vertical

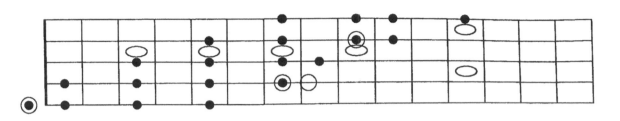

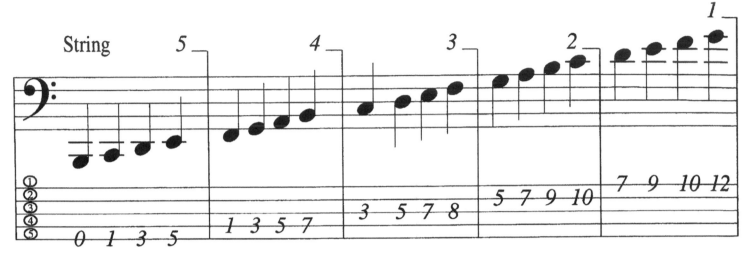

Ex.3 Horizontal / Vertical

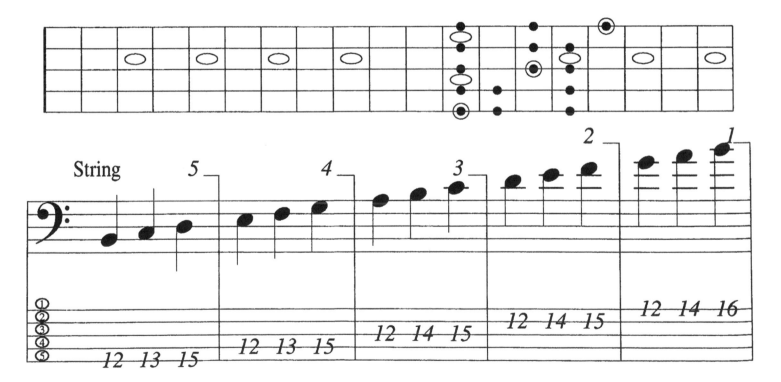

26

(KEY OF B)

B Ionian

Ex. 1 Horizontal

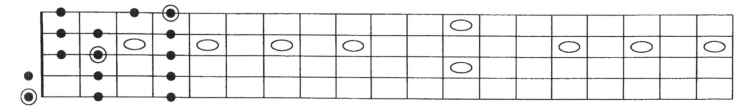

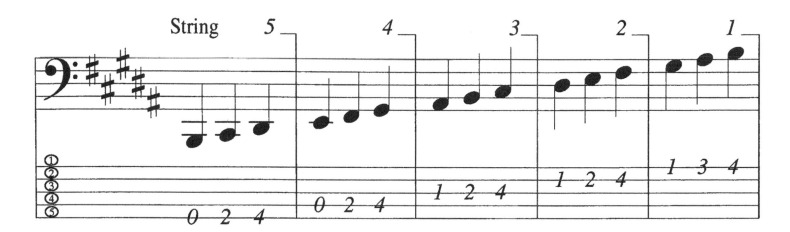

Ex. 2 Vertical

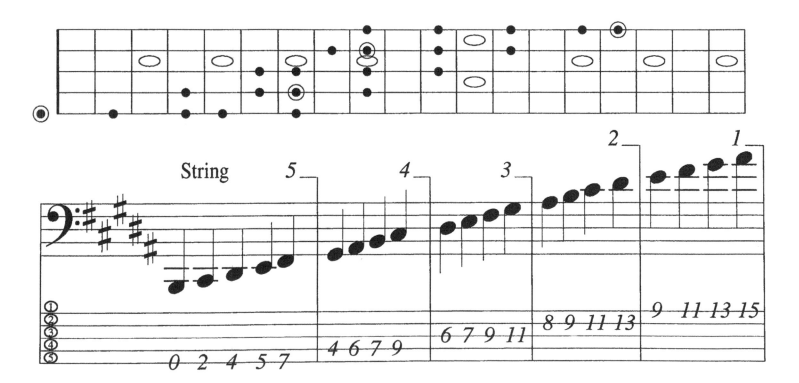

Ex. 3 Horizontal / Vertical

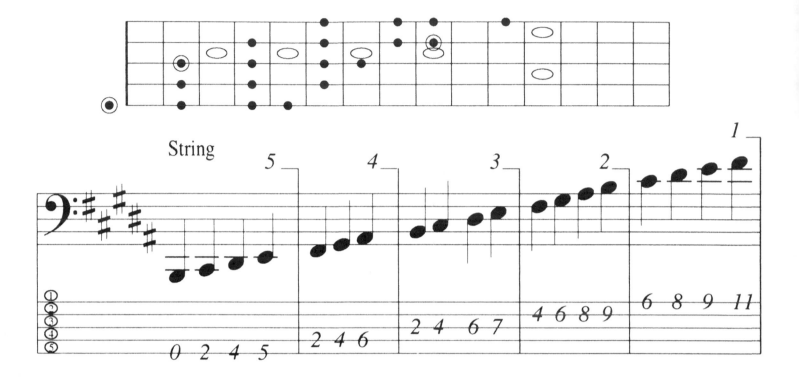

String

5   4   3   2   1

0 2 4 5   2 4 6   2 4 6 7   4 6 8 9   6 8 9 11

Rocky Thacker

C# Dorian

Ex.1 Horizontal

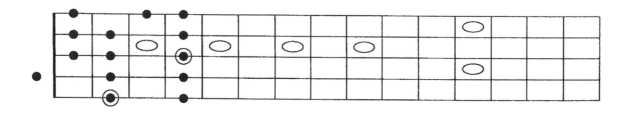

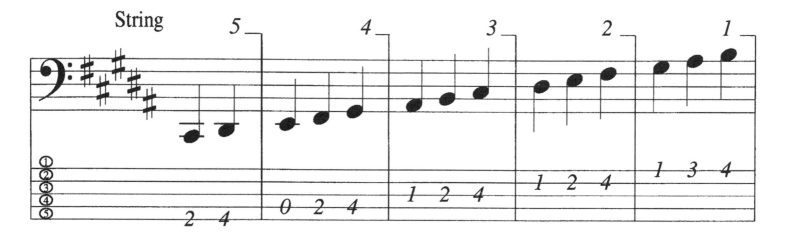

Ex. 2 Vertical

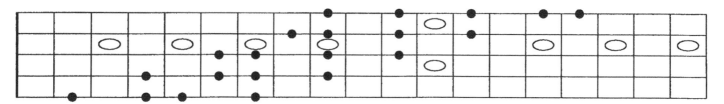

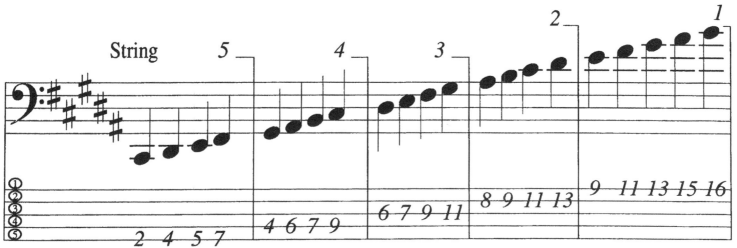

Ex.3 Horizontal / Vertical

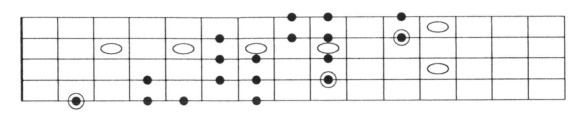

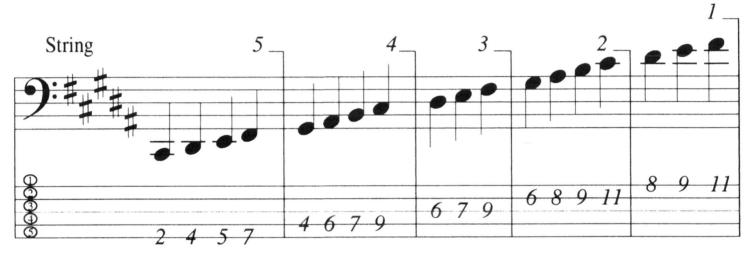

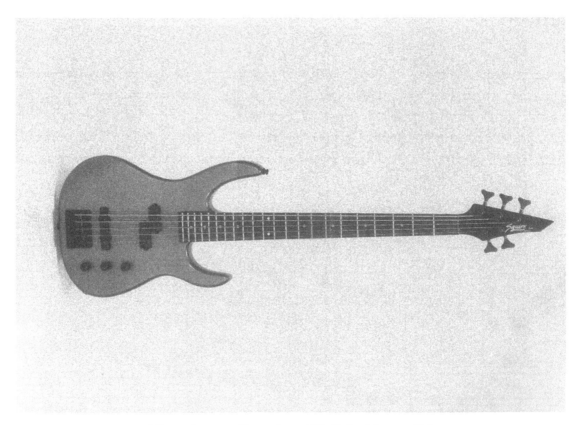

Fender - Squier H.M. Bass V

D# Phrygian

Ex.1 Horizontal

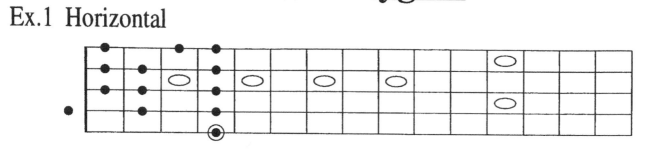

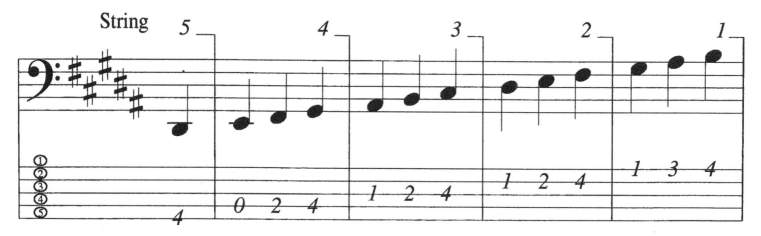

Ex.2 Vertical

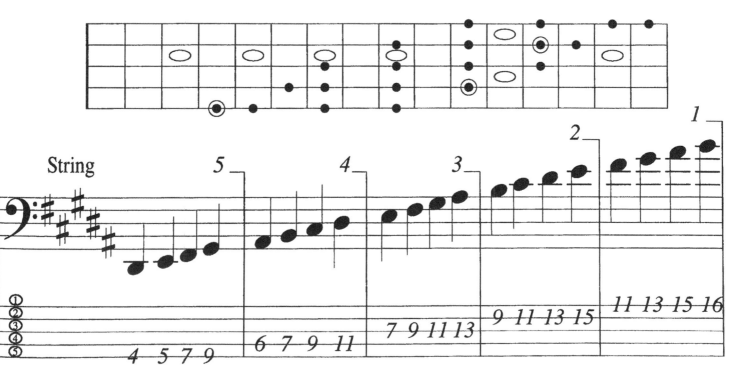

31

Ex. 3 Horizontal / Vertical

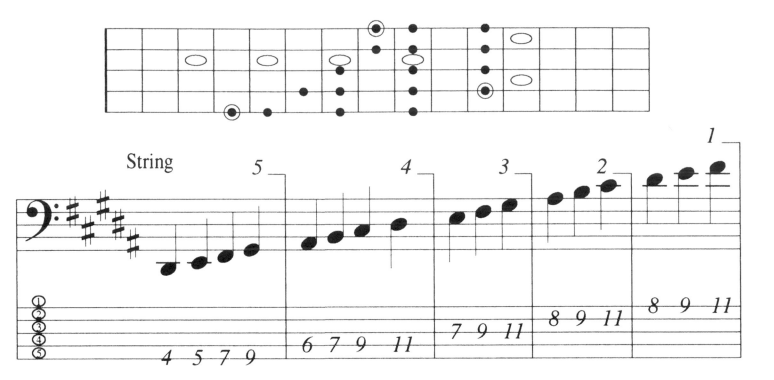

Denny Dadmun - Bixby

E Lydian

Ex.1 Horizontal

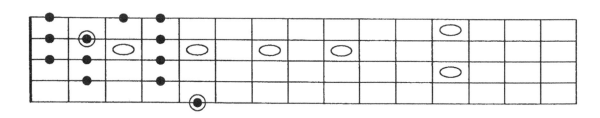

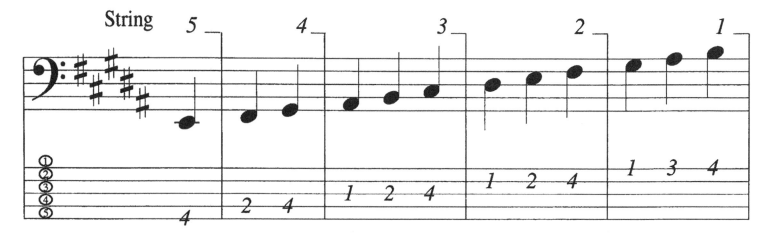

Ex.2 Vertical

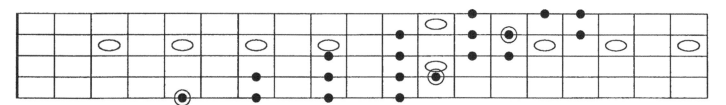

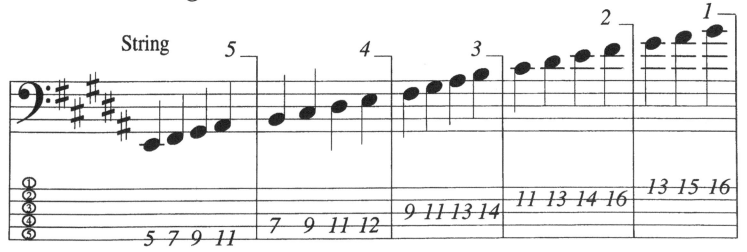

Ex. 3 Horizontal / Vertical

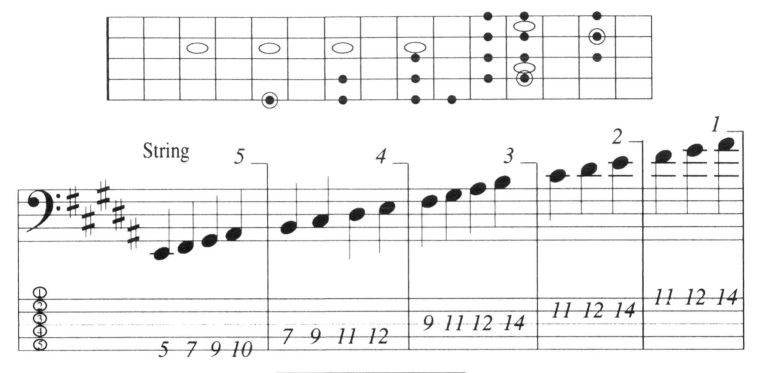

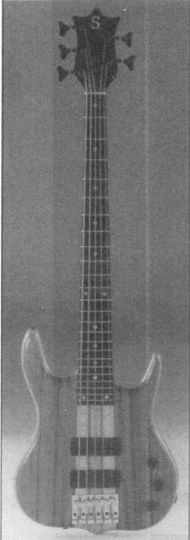

Ken Smith - B.T. Custom V "G"

F# Mixolydian

Ex. 1 Horizontal

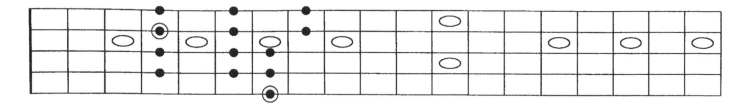

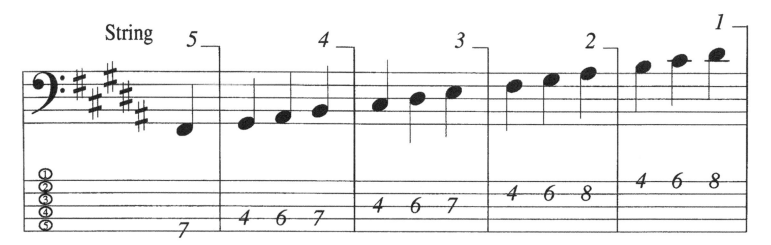

Ex. 2 Vertical

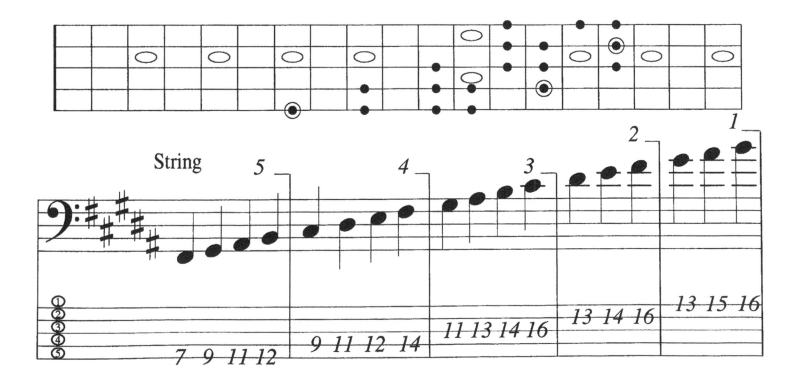

Ex. 3 Horizontal / Vertical

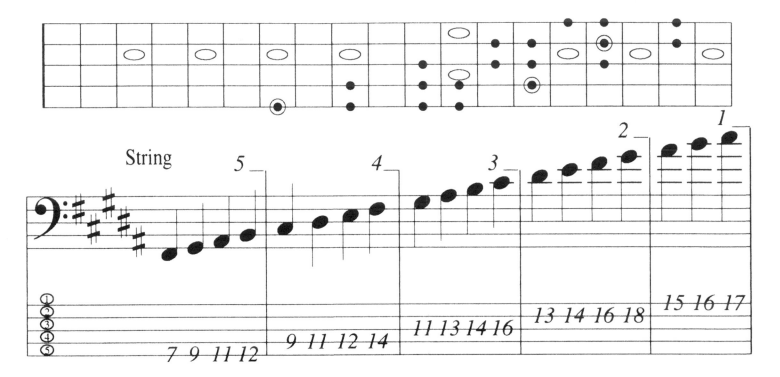

Dave Freeman

G# Aeolian

Ex. 1 Horizontal

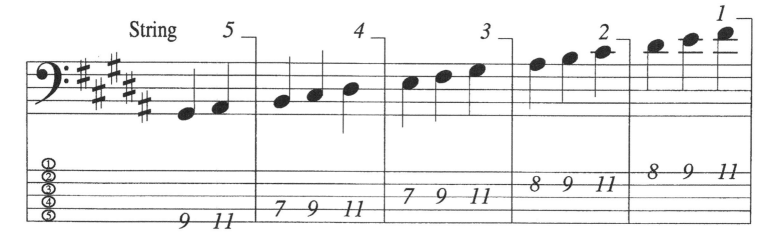

Ex. 2 Vertical

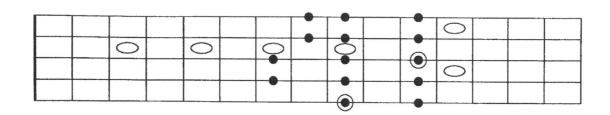

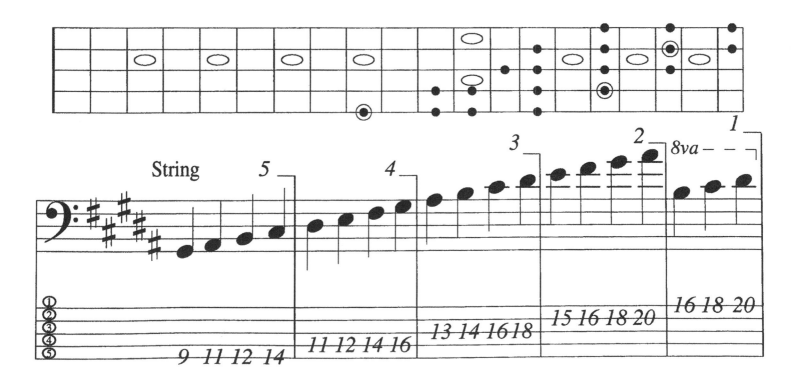

Ex. 3 Horizontal / Vertical

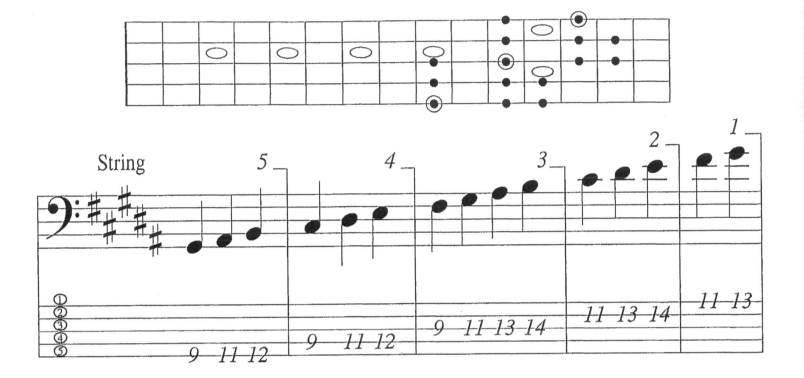

String

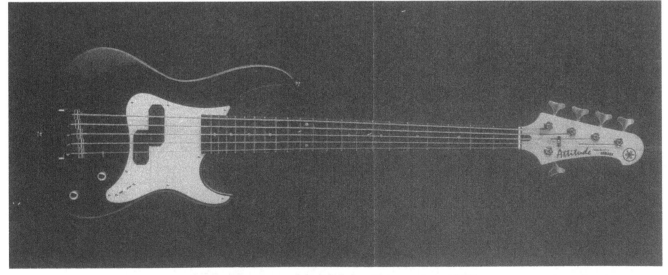

Yamaha - Attitude Standard 5

A# Locrian

Ex. 1 Horizontal

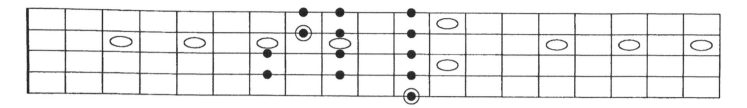

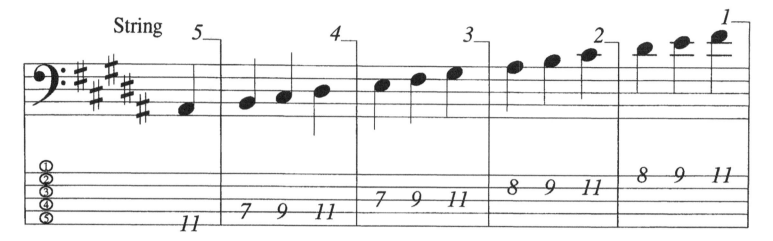

Ex. 2 Vertical

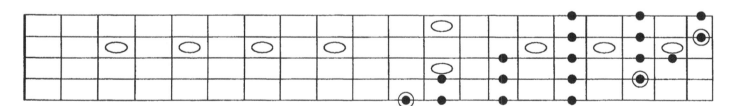

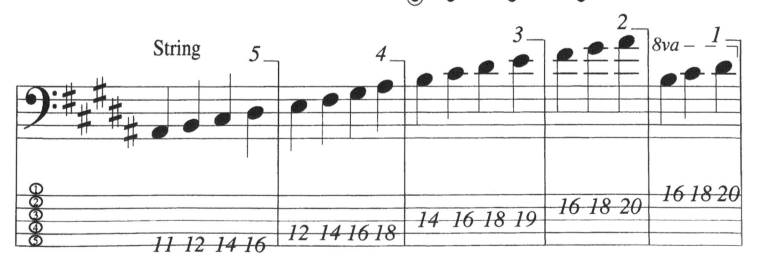

39

Ex. 3 Horizontal / Vertical

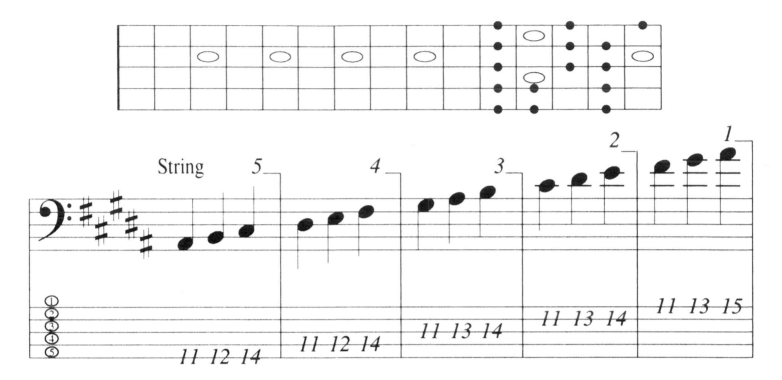

String

11 12 14

11 12 14

11 13 14

11 13 14

11 13 15

Allen Woody
PHOTO: Courtesy of Steinberger

Ionian Modes

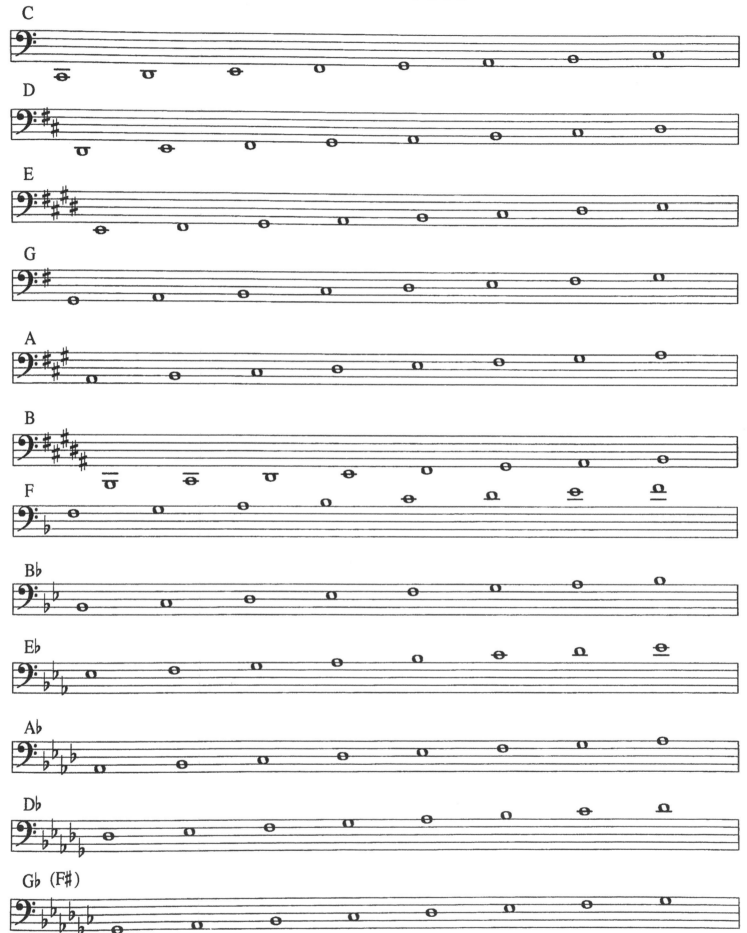

C

D

E

G

A

B

F

B♭

E♭

A♭

D♭

G♭ (F♯)

Dorian Modes

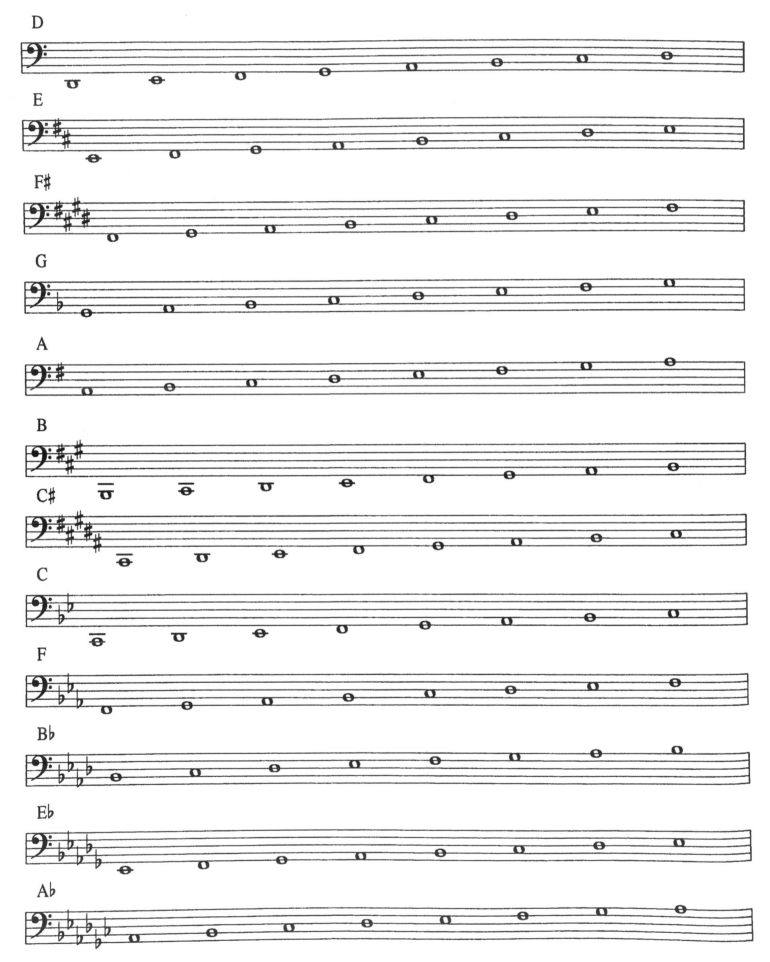

Phrygian Modes

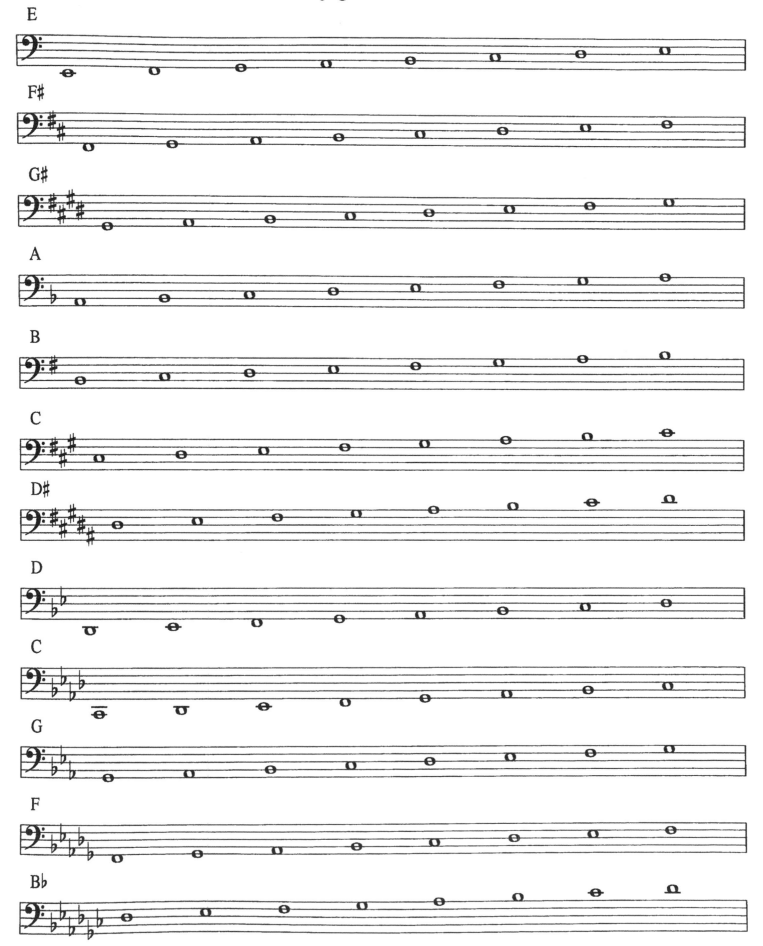

Lydian Modes

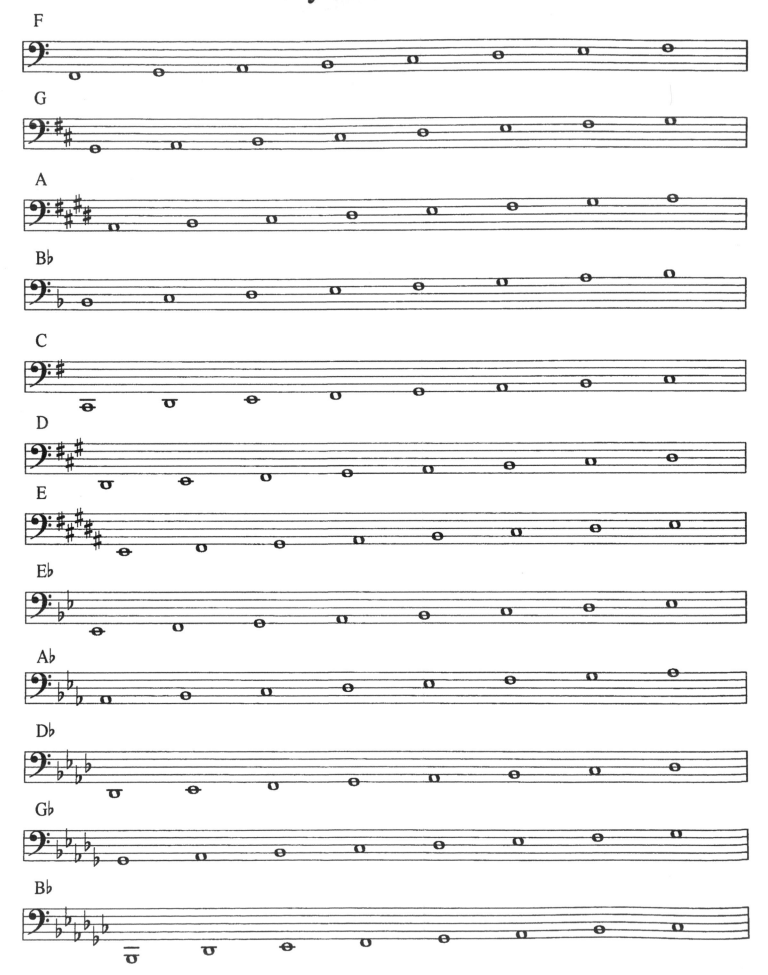

Mixolydian Modes

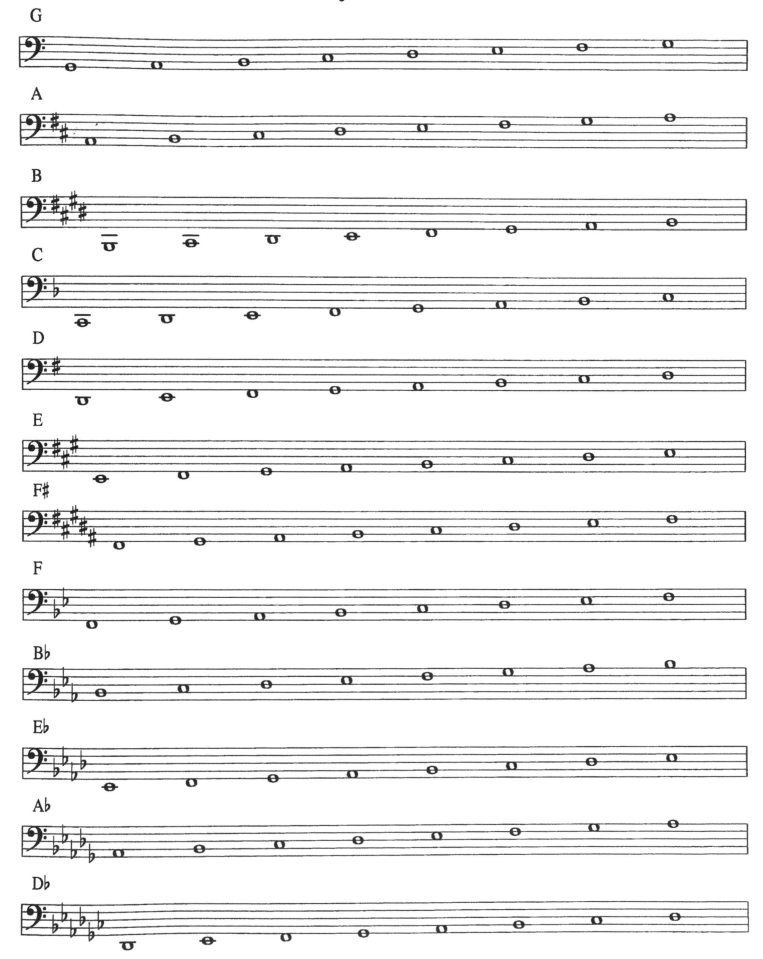

Aeolian Modes

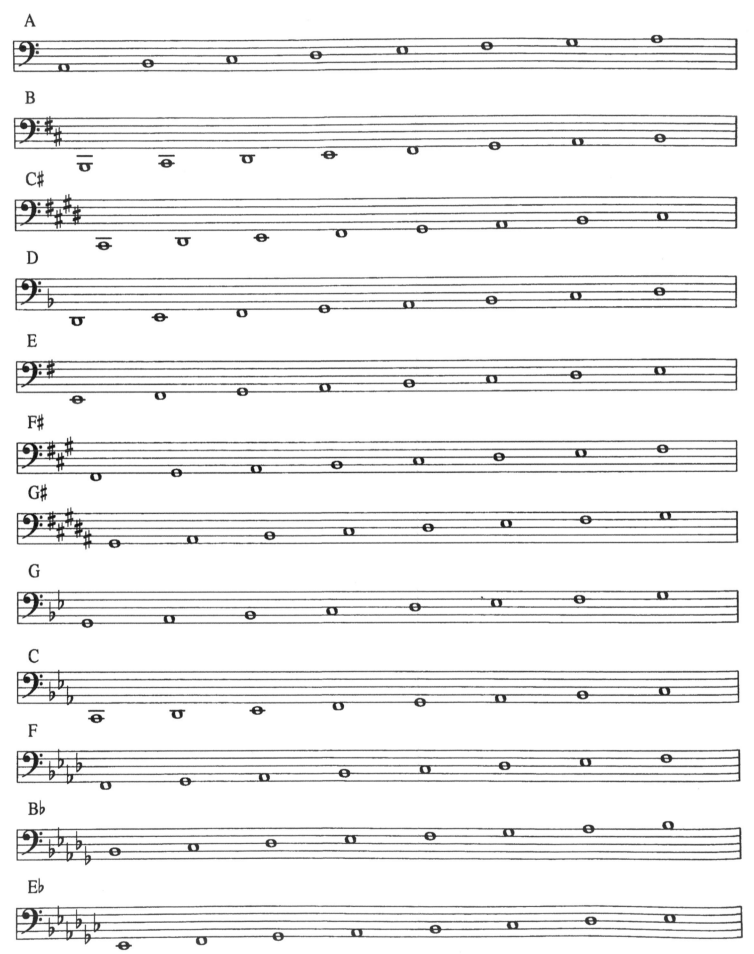

Locrian Modes

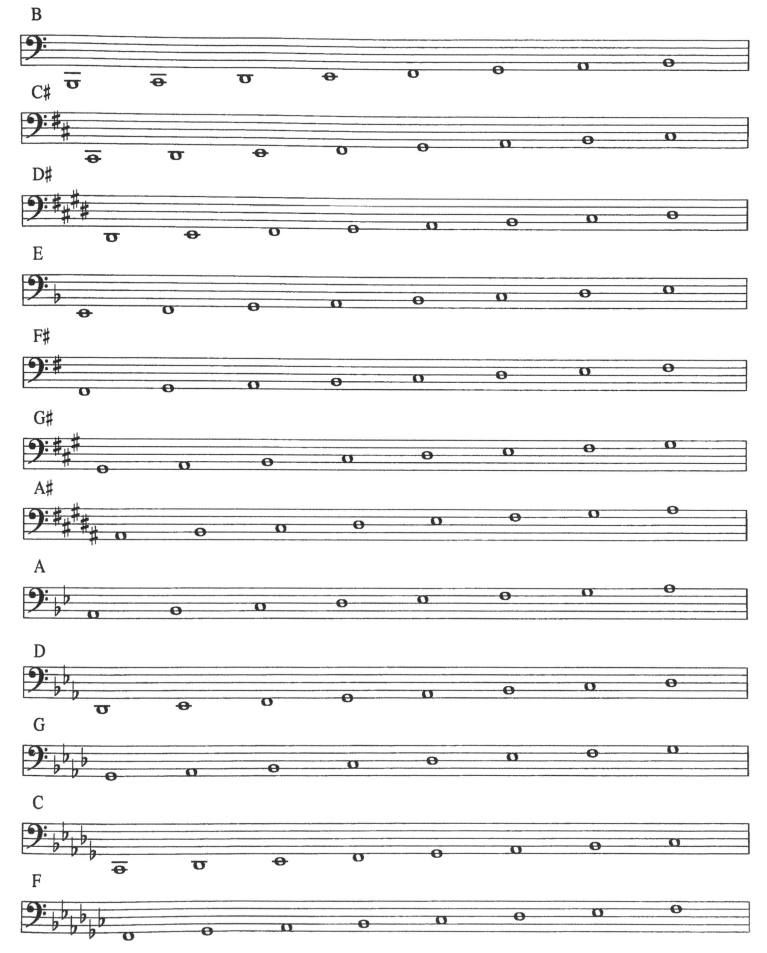

HARMONIC MINOR SCALE

The harmonic minor scale is constructed off the sixth degree of the major scale. We see from the illustrated example that C harmonic minor is related to Eb major scale.

The seventh step in the harmonic minor is raised one half step. It's this interval skip of an augmented second (minor 3rd) that makes this scale different from the natural or melodic minor scale.

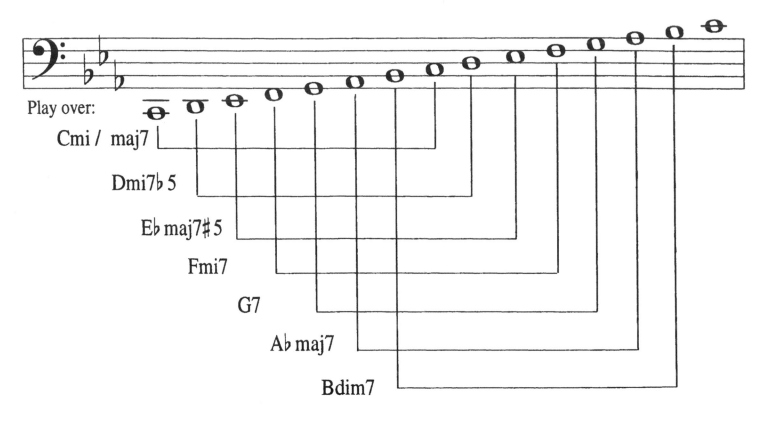

Play over:

Cmi / maj7

Dmi7b 5

Eb maj7♯5

Fmi7

G7

Ab maj7

Bdim7

Harmonic Minor plays over;

1) Any minor 7b5 chord; one whole step down or minor 7 interval from root of that chord.
   i.e. E minor 7b5=D harmonic minor scale.

2) Any minor 7 chord; on the 5th interval from the root of that chord.
   i.e. F minor 7=C harmonic minor scale.

3) Any minor 7 chord; on the major 3rd interval from the root of that chord.
   i.e. C major 7=E harmonic minor scale.

4) Any diminished chord; on the minor 2nd interval from the root of that chord.
   i.e. C# diminished=D harmonic minor scale.

5) Any dominant chord with a b9 or b13 (#5); on the perfect 4th interval from the root of that chord.
   i.e. A7#5b9=D harmonic minor scale

6) Any dominant chord with a #9 and a #11; on the perfect 5th interval from the root of that chord.
   i.e. F7#9 or #11=C harmonic minor scale.

C Harmonic Minor

Ex. 1 Horizontal

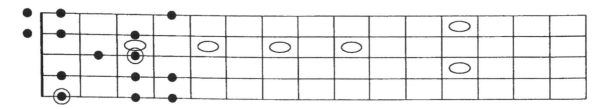

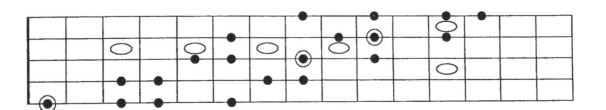

Ex.2 Vertical

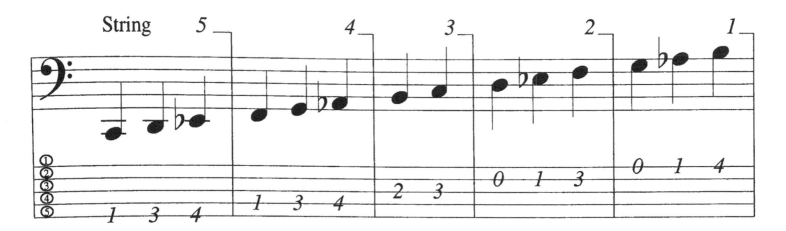

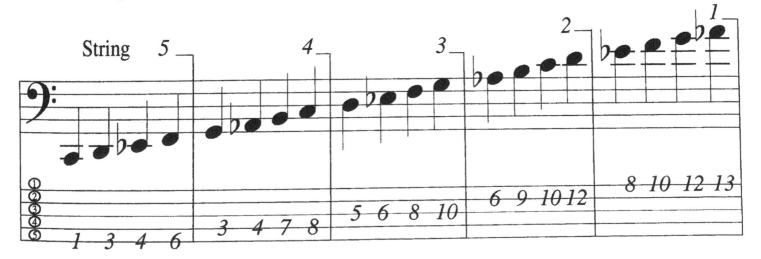

Ex. 3 Horizontal / Vertical

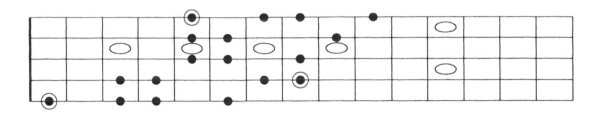

String

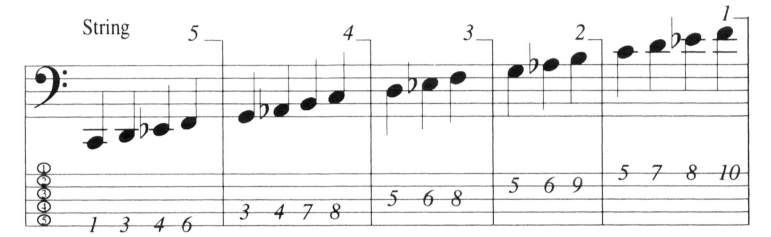

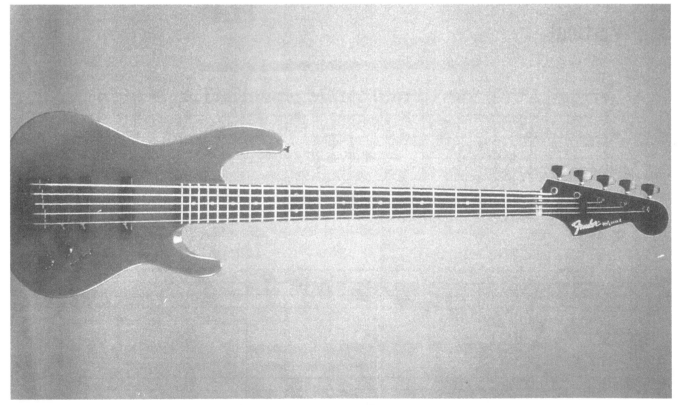

Fender - H.N. Bass V

B Harmonic Minor

Ex. 1 Horizontal

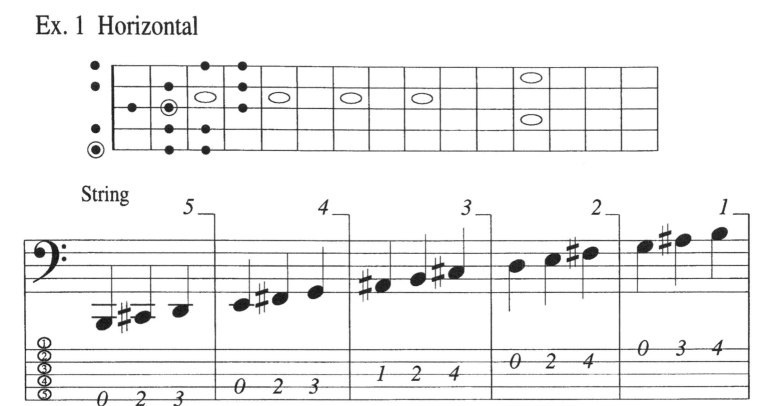

String

Ex. 2 Vertical

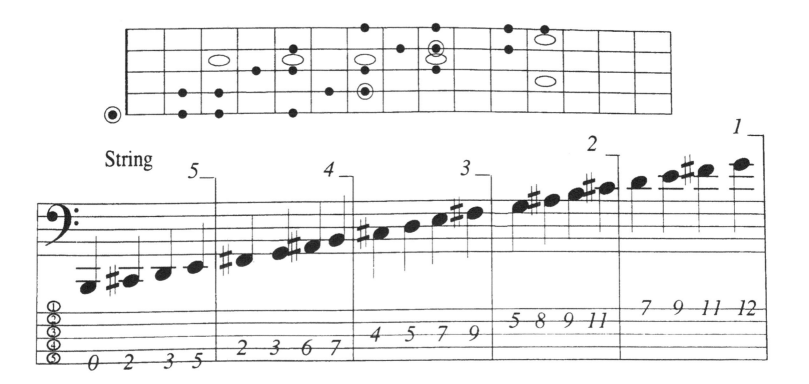

String

Ex. 3 Horizontal / Vertical

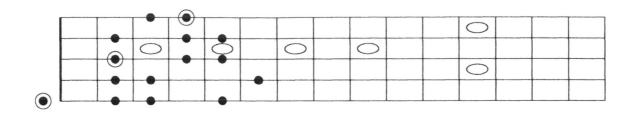

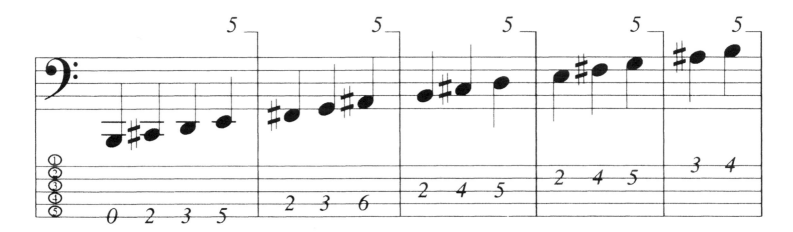

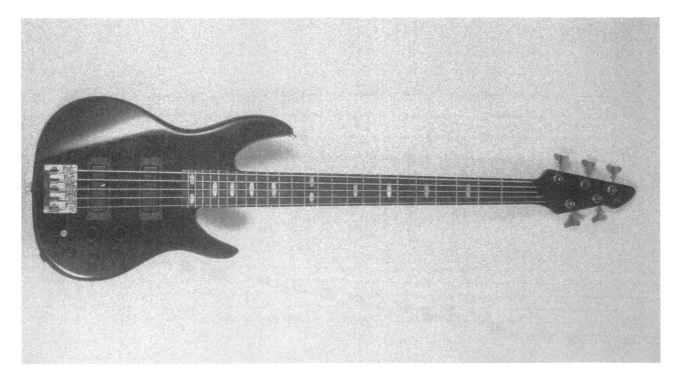

Peavey - TL-Five

Harmonic Minor Scales

MAJOR PENTATONIC SCALES

Pentatonic Scales are five note scales made up of major seconds and minor thirds, having no leading tone or seventh scale degree of a major scale. There are no half steps which make the scale very interchangeable.

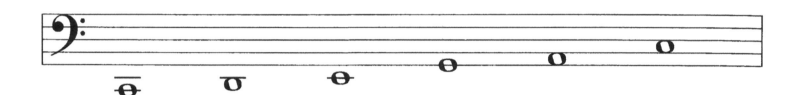

Major Pentatonic plays over;

1) Any major chord unaltered; i.e. C Major7, C Major6, C Major6/9=C Major Pentatonic

2) Any suspended four chord; i.e. C sus4=C Major Pentatonic

3) Any dominant seven chord; i.e. C7=C Major Pentatonic

4) Any altered dominant seven chord (b5, #5, b9, #9) on the flat 5 of that chord;
   i.e. C7b5, C7#5, C7b9, C7#9, C7b5#9=Gb Major Pentatonic.

C Major Pentatonic

Ex. 1 Horizontal

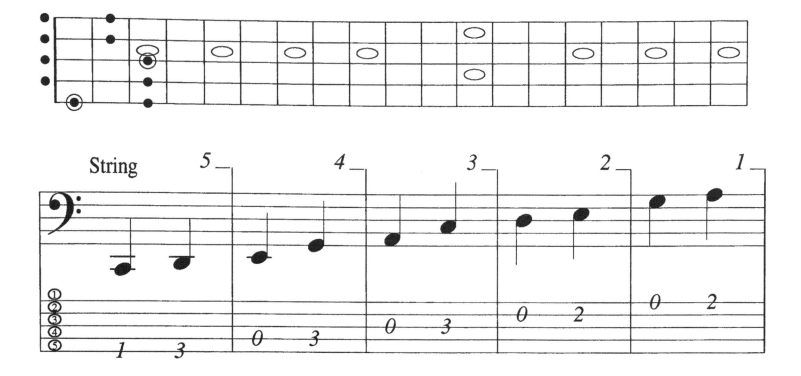

Ex. 2 Vertical

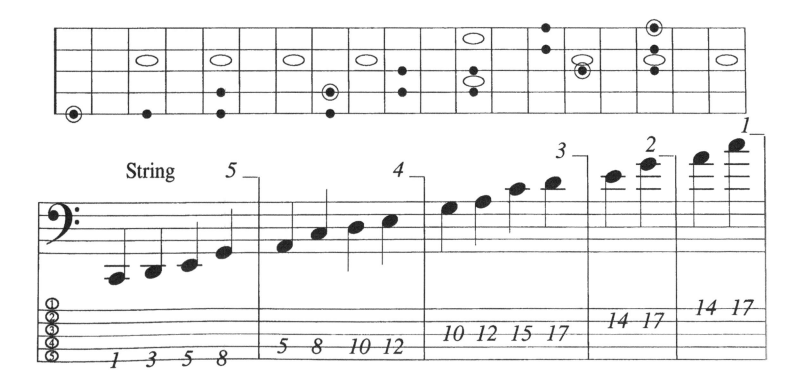

Ex. 3 Horizontal / Vertical

Morty Black

PHOTO: Lars Botten/Courtesy of Mike Caron

B Major Pentatonic

Ex. 1 Horizontal

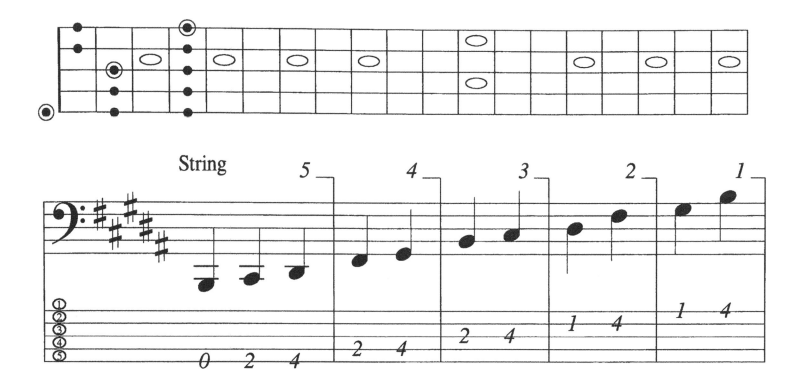

Ex. 2 Vertical

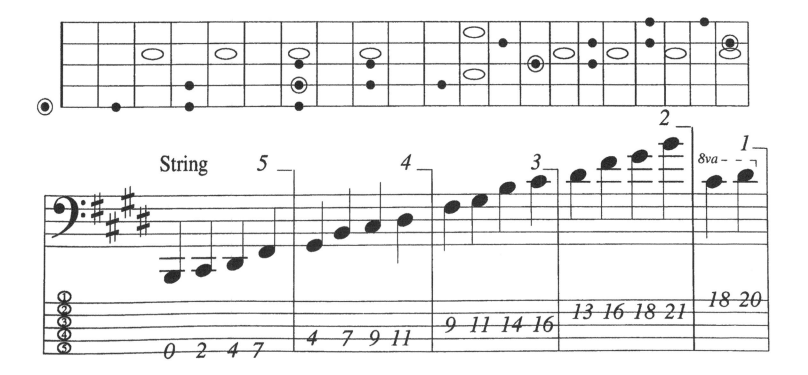

Ex. 2 Vertical

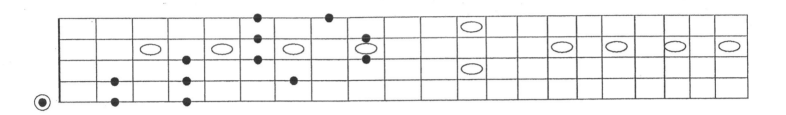

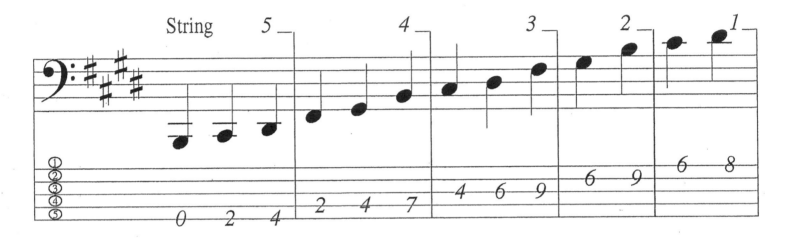

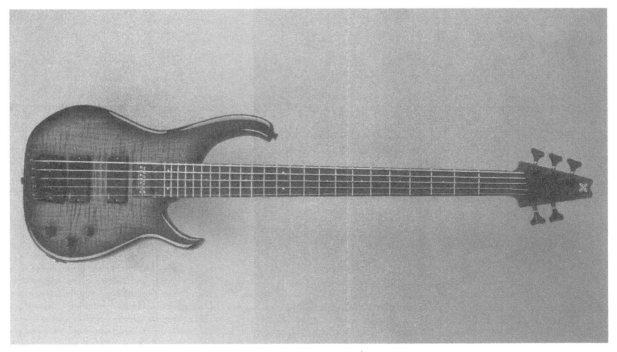

Modulus Quantum 5 SPi

Major Pentatonic Scales

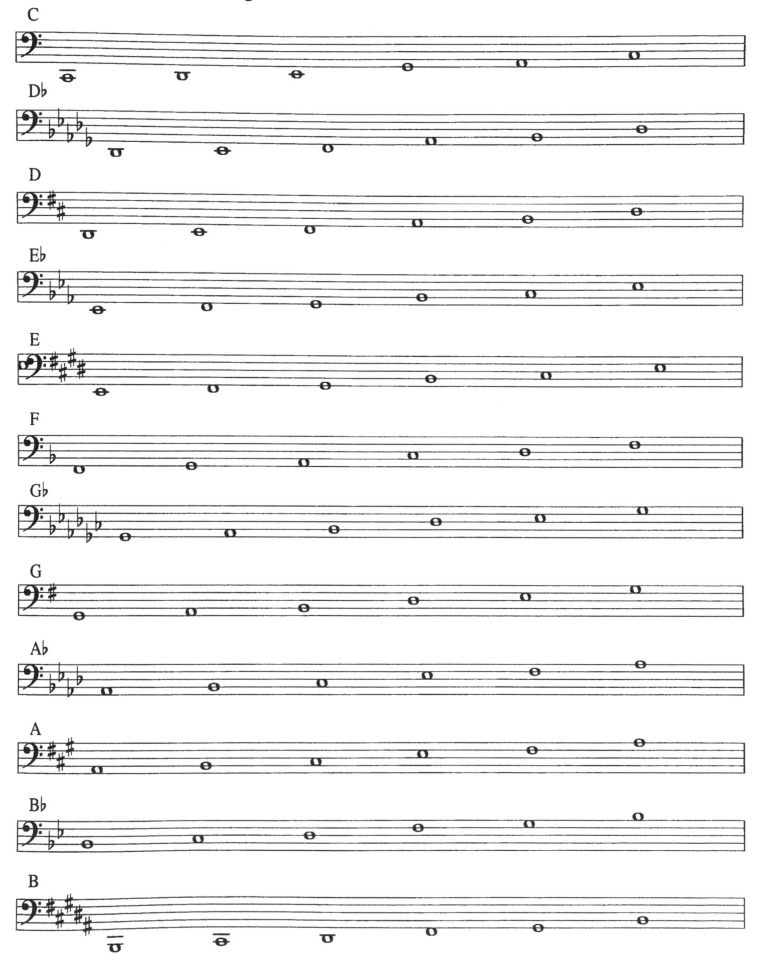

Minor Pentatonic Scales

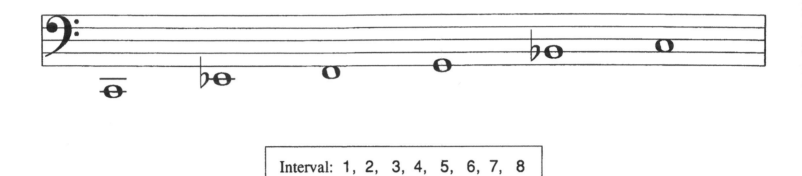

```
Interval: 1, 2, 3, 4, 5, 6, 7, 8
Key:      C, D, E, F, G, A, B, C
```

Minor Pentatonic plays over;

1) Any minor chord; i.e. C minor, C minor7, Cminor7sus4, C minor9, C minor11, C minor13=
   C minor pentatonic

2) Any minor seven chord on the 5th; i.e. C minor7, C minor7sus4=G minor pentatonic

3) Any major chord; i.e. C Major=C minor pentatonic

4) Any major seven chord on the 3rd; i.e. C major7=E minor pentatonic

5) Any major seven chord on the 7th; i.e. C major7=B minor pentatonic

6) Any major seven flat five chord on the 7th; i.e. C major7b5=B minor pentatonic

7) Any major chord with a suspended 4th; i.e. Csus4=D minor pentatonic

8) Any dominant seven sharp nine chord; i.e. C7#9=C minor pentatonic

9) Any dominant seven with an altered 5th or 9th on the b3rd
      i.e. C7b5, C7#5, C7b9, C7#9, C7b5#9=Eb minor pentatonic

10) Any dominant seven suspended four chord on the 2nd; i.e. C7sus4=D minor pentatonic

11) Any dominant seven suspended four chord on the 5th; i.e. C7sus4=G minor pentatonic

C Minor Pentatonic

Ex. 1 Horizontal

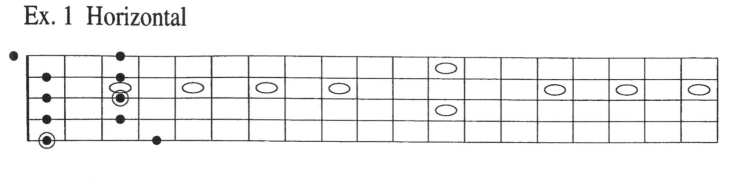

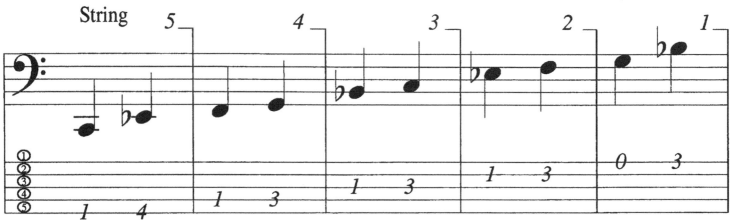

Ex. 2 Vertical

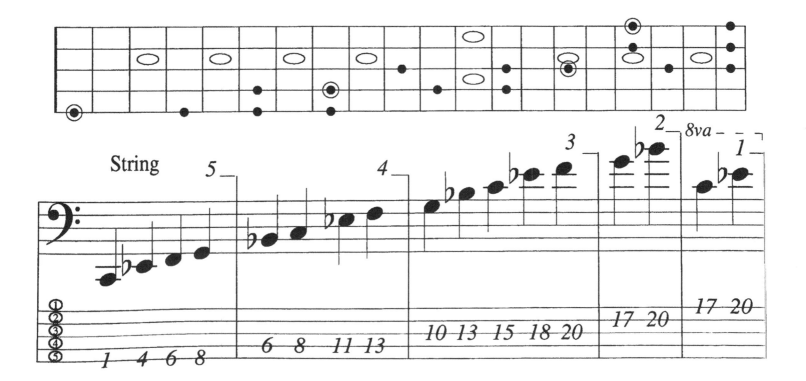

Ex. 3 Horizontal / Vertical

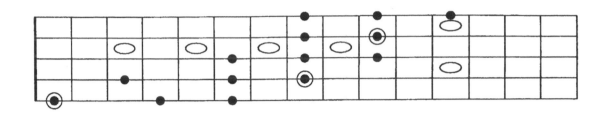

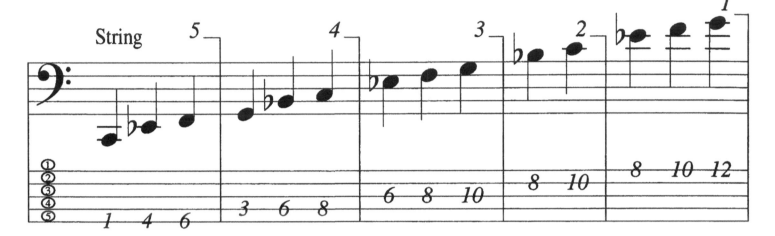

B Minor Pentatonic

Ex. 1 Horizontal

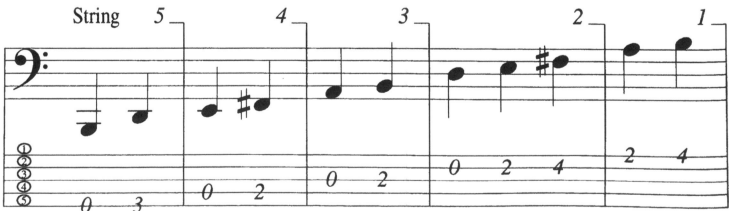

Ex. 2 Vertical

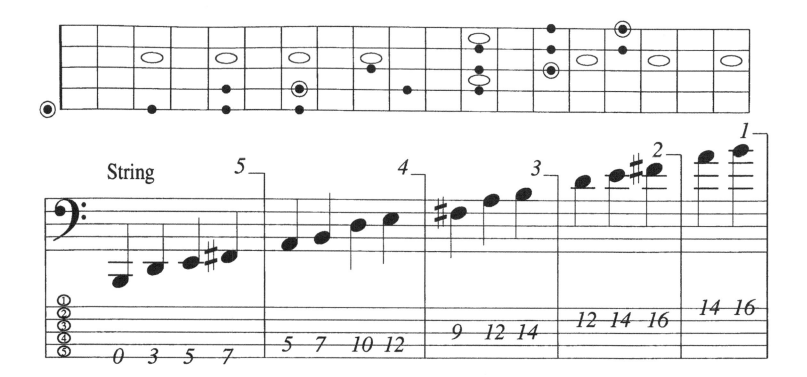

Ex. 3 Horizontal / Vertical

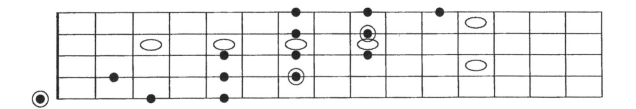

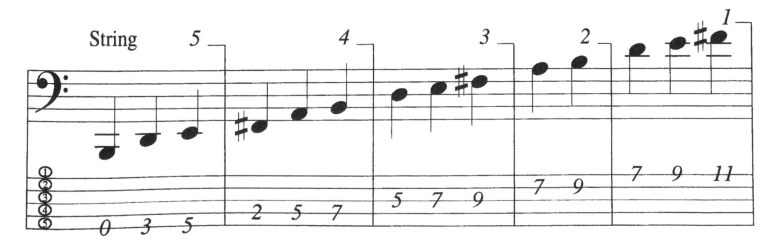

Minor Pentatonic Scales

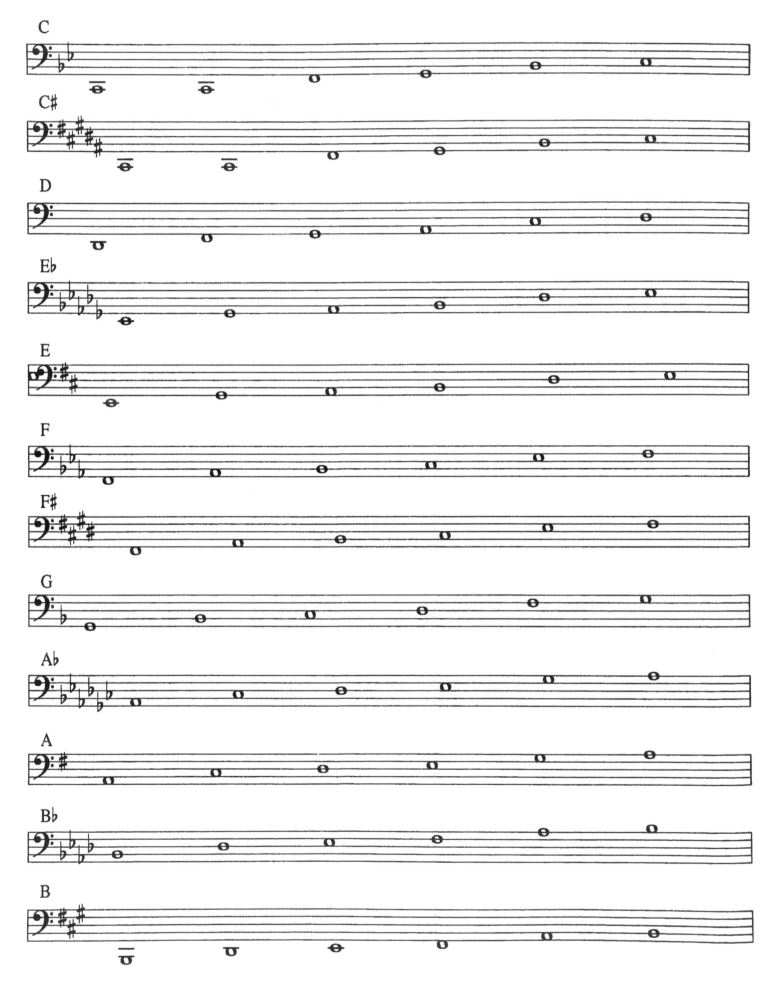

BLUES SCALE

The Blues Scale is constructed of two whole steps, two half steps and two minor third steps.

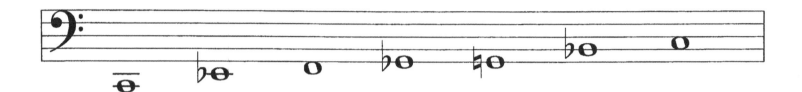

Blues plays over;

1) Any minor seven chord; i.e. C minor7=C blues

2) Any minor six or six/nine chord; i.e. C minor6/9=C blues

3) Any minor seven as a two chord; i.e. Key of C=D blues

4) Any dominant seven sharp nine chord; i.e. C7#9=C blues

C Blues

Ex.1 Horizontal

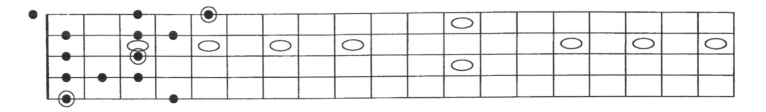

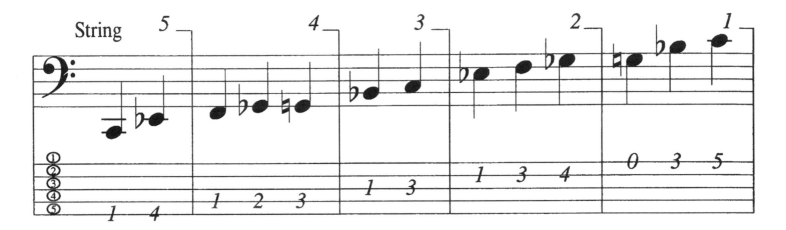

Ex. 2 Vertical

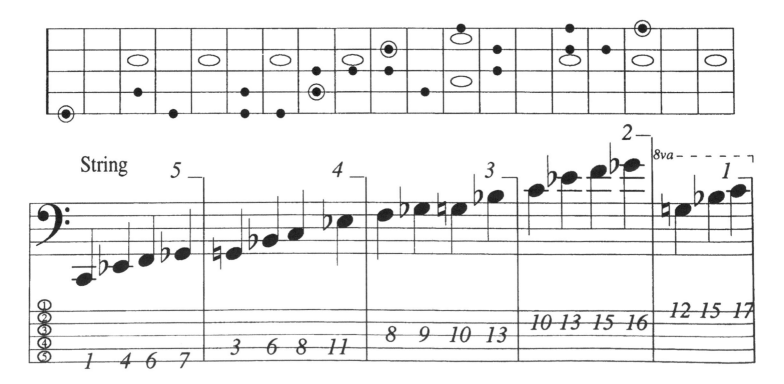

Ex.3 Horizontal / Vertical

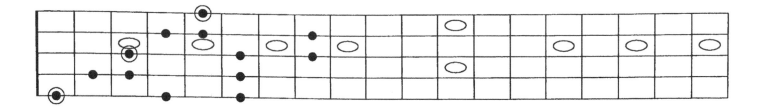

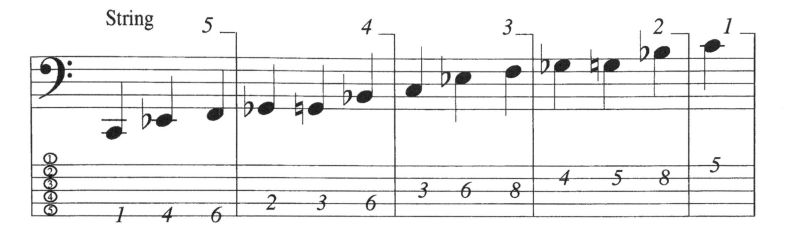

B Blues

Ex. 1 Horizontal

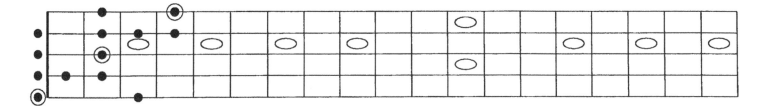

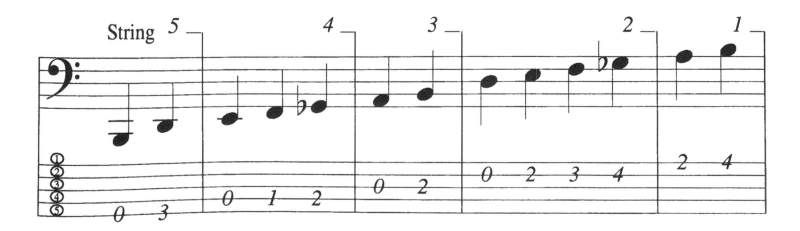

Ex. 2 Vertical

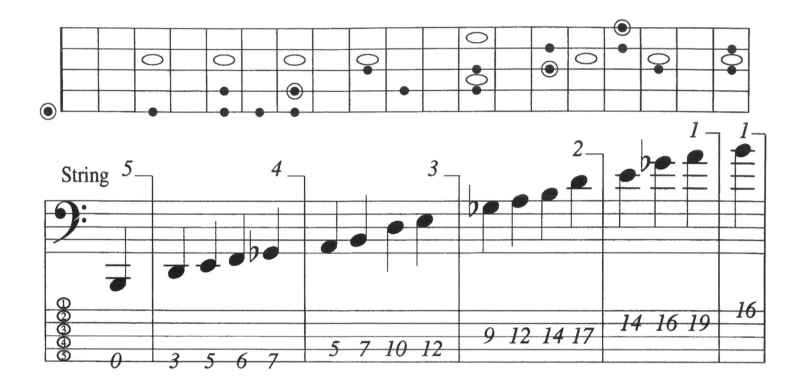

Ex. 3 Horizontal / Vertical

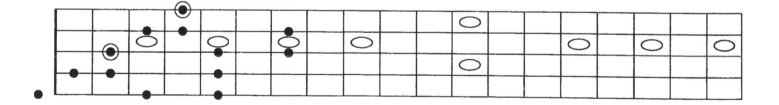

68

Blues Scales

MELODIC MINOR SCALES

DEFINITION: An altered natural minor scale, the melodic minor scale is constructed of five whole steps and two half steps.

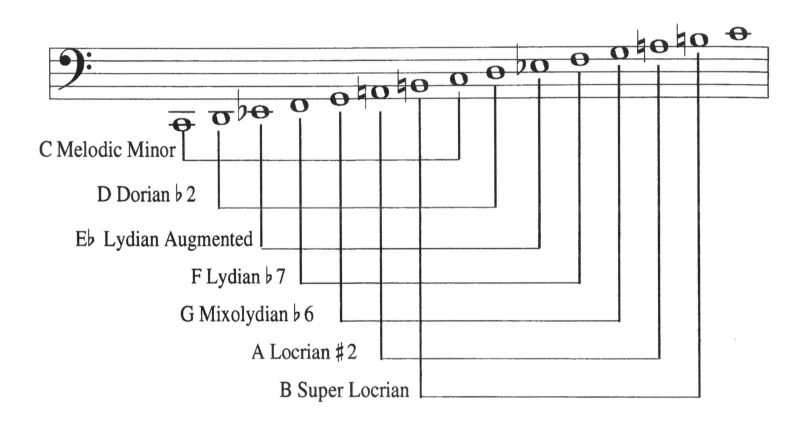

C Melodic Minor

D Dorian ♭2

E♭ Lydian Augmented

F Lydian ♭7

G Mixolydian ♭6

A Locrian ♯2

B Super Locrian

Melodic Minor plays over;

1) Any minor six or six/nine chord; i.e. Cminor6/9=C melodic minor

C Melodic Minor

Ex. 1 Horizontal

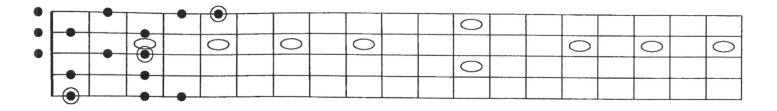

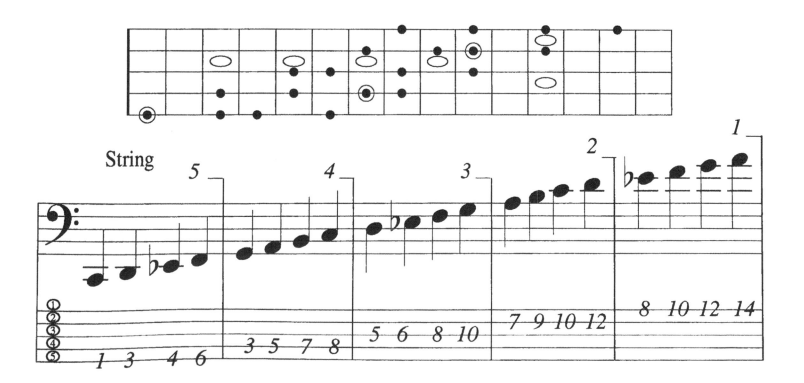

Ex. 2 Vertical

Ex. 1 Horizontal / Vertical

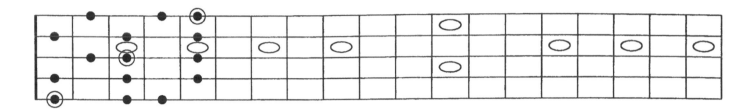

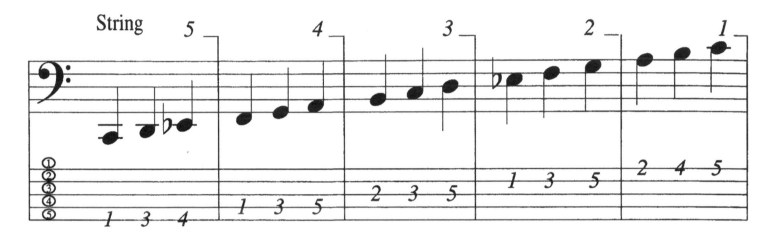

B Melodic Minor

Ex. 1 Horizontal

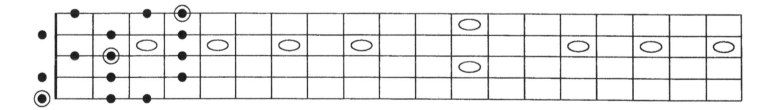

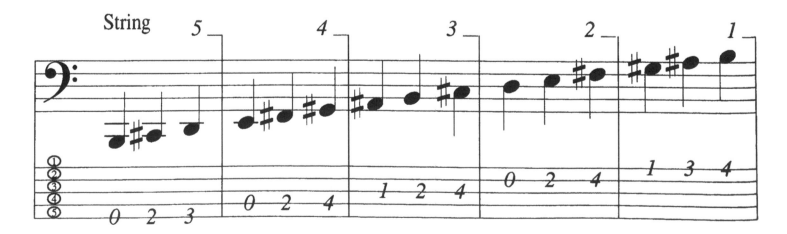

Ex. 2 Vertical

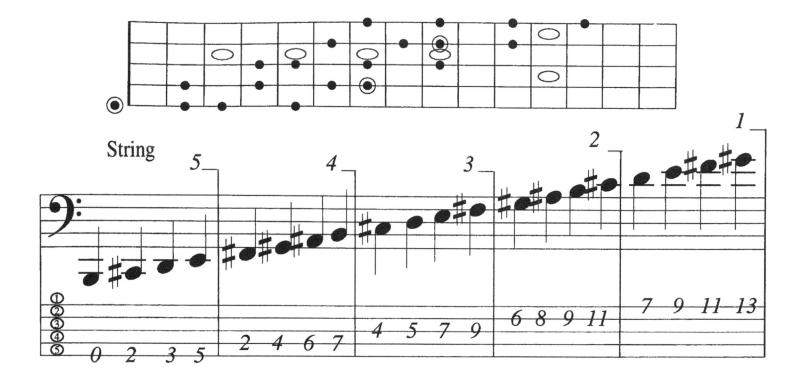

Ex. 1 Horizontal / Vertical

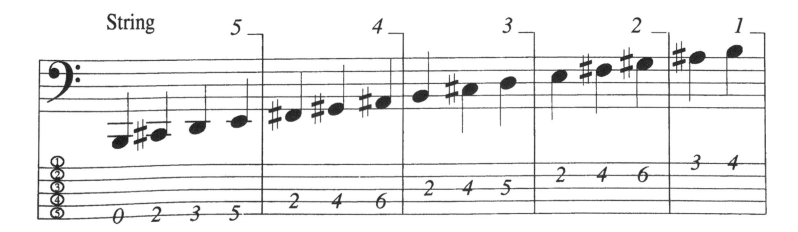

Melodic Minor Scales

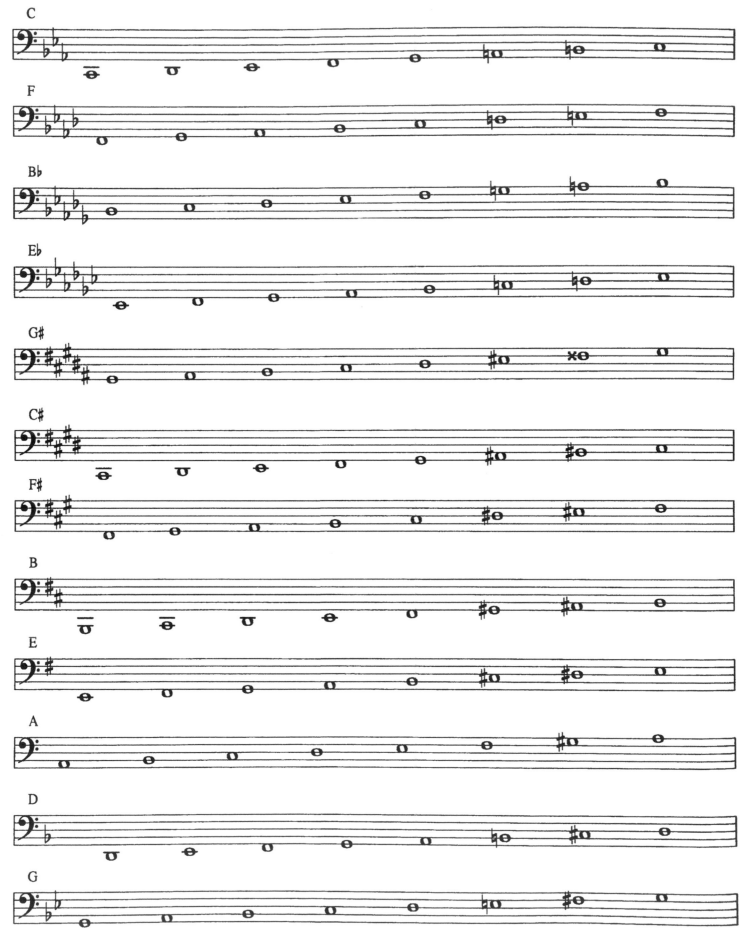

THE CHROMATIC SCALE

The chromatic scale is constructed of all half steps.
There is only one chromatic scale which can begin on any tone.

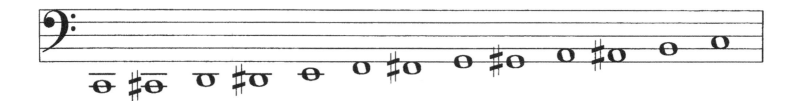

Chromatic scale plays over:

1) Any chord type with any alterations. Some of the scale tones will always
be dissonant, to the harmony and will have a strong tendency to move either
up or down a half step to the nearest chord tone.

Chromatic Scale

Ex. 1 Horizontal

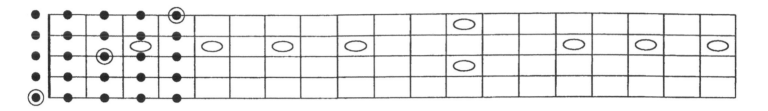

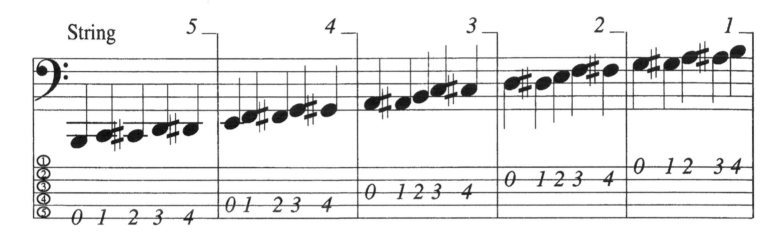

String

5   4   3   2   1

0 1 2 3 4   0 1 2 3 4   0 1 2 3 4   0 1 2 3 4   0 1 2 3 4

Ex. 2 Vertical

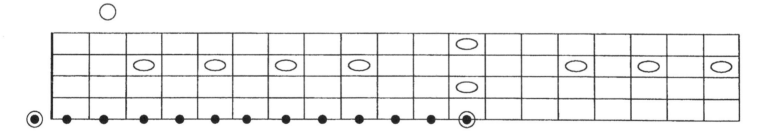

String

0 1 2 3 4 5 6 7 8 9 10 11 12 13 14 15 16 17 18 19 20

Contrary Motion Exercise
This exercise has two scales moving in opposite directions

Ex. 3

Chromatic Scale

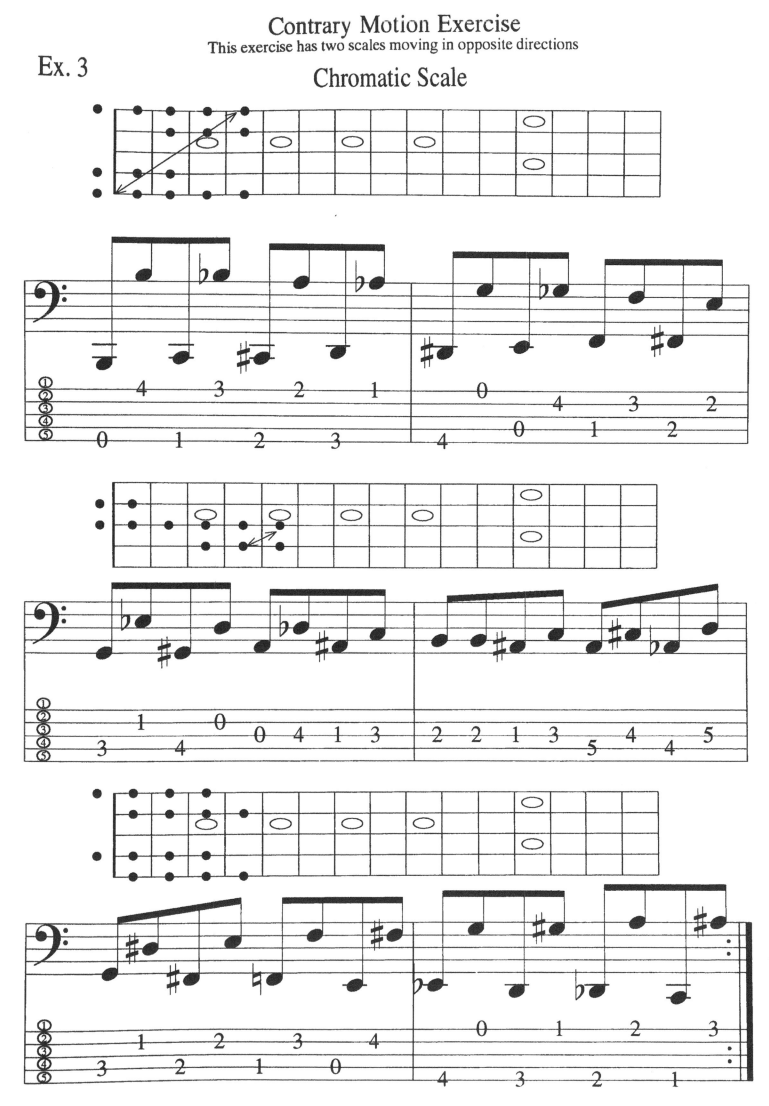

WHOLE TONE SCALE

Constructed exclusively of whole steps, six in all.
Since there are only twelve tones in the chromatic scale, then there are only two different sounding whole tone scales.
Each of those two scales can be interpreted enharmonically as several different scales.

Whole Tone plays over;

1) Any dominant seven flat five or sharp five; i.e. C7b5, C7#5=C wholetone

2) Any dominant seven altered 5th or 9th; i.e. C7b5, C7#9, C7#5, C7b9, C7b5#9=C whole tone

3) Any augmented chord; i.e. C Augmented=C whole tone

C Whole Tone Scale

Ex. 1 Horizontal

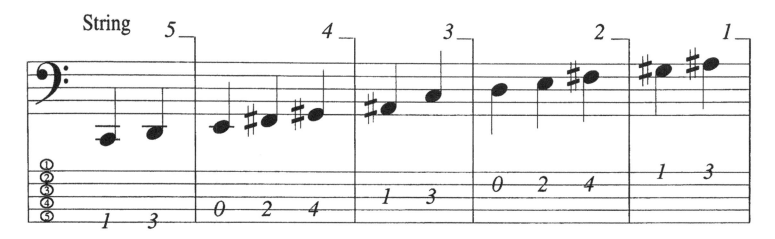

Ex. 2 Vertical

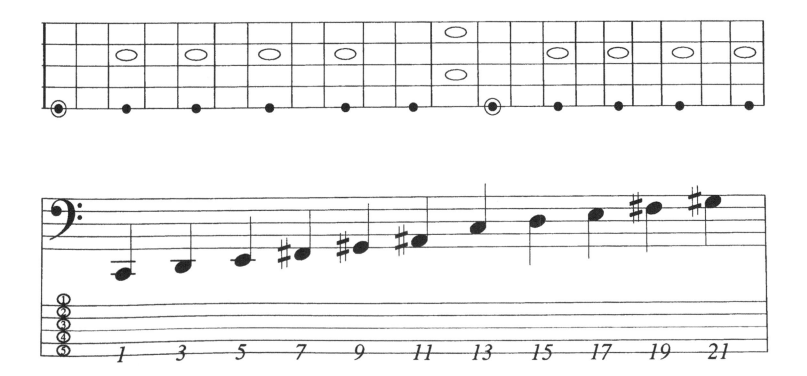

Whole Tone Scales

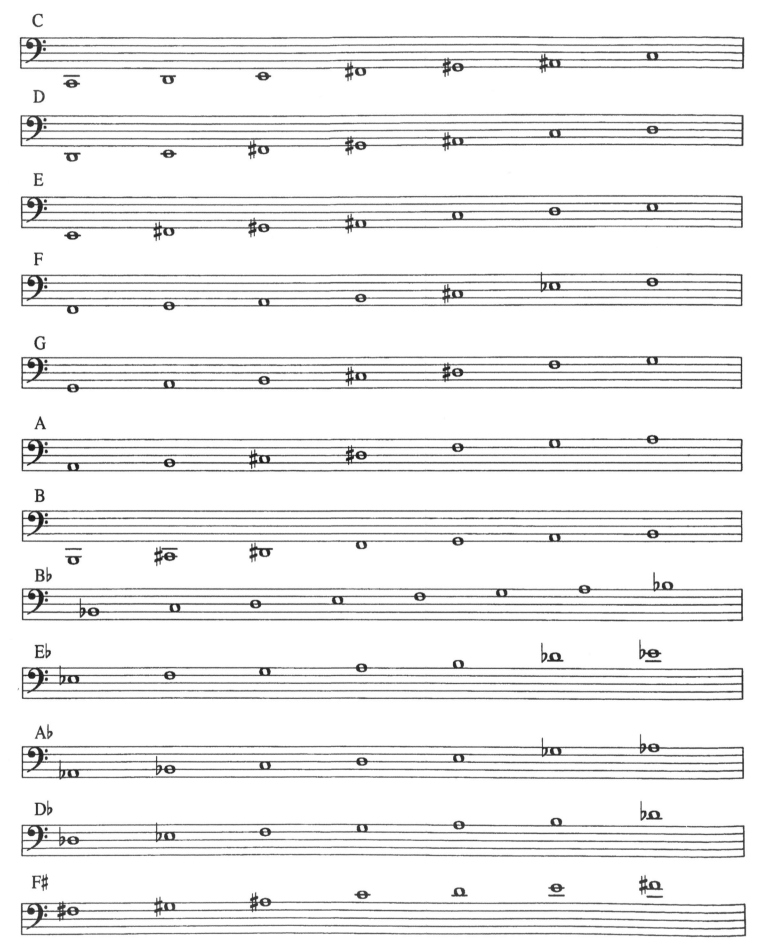

WHOLE-HALF STEP
DIMINISHED SCALE

Whole to Half step diminished plays over;

1) Any half diminished chord; i..e. Cminor7b5=C whole/half step diminished

2) Any fully diminished chor; i.e. Cdim,7=C whole/half step diminished

C Diminished Scale
(Whole to Half Step)

Ex. 1 Horizontal

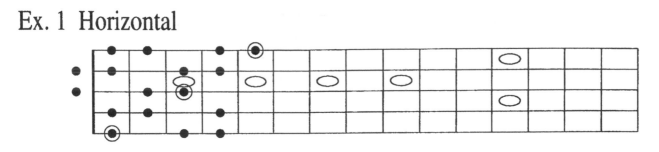

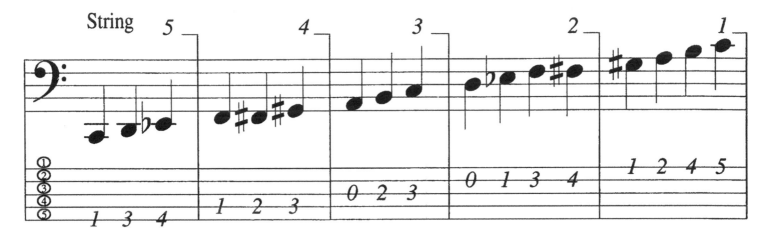

Ex. 2 Vertical

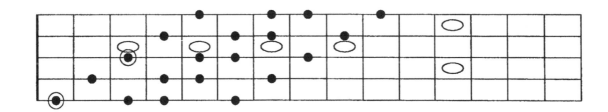

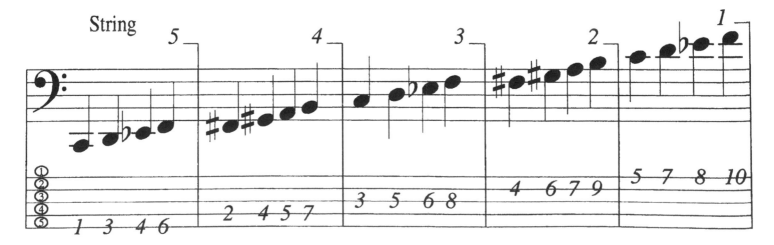

Diminished Scales
(Whole to Half Step)

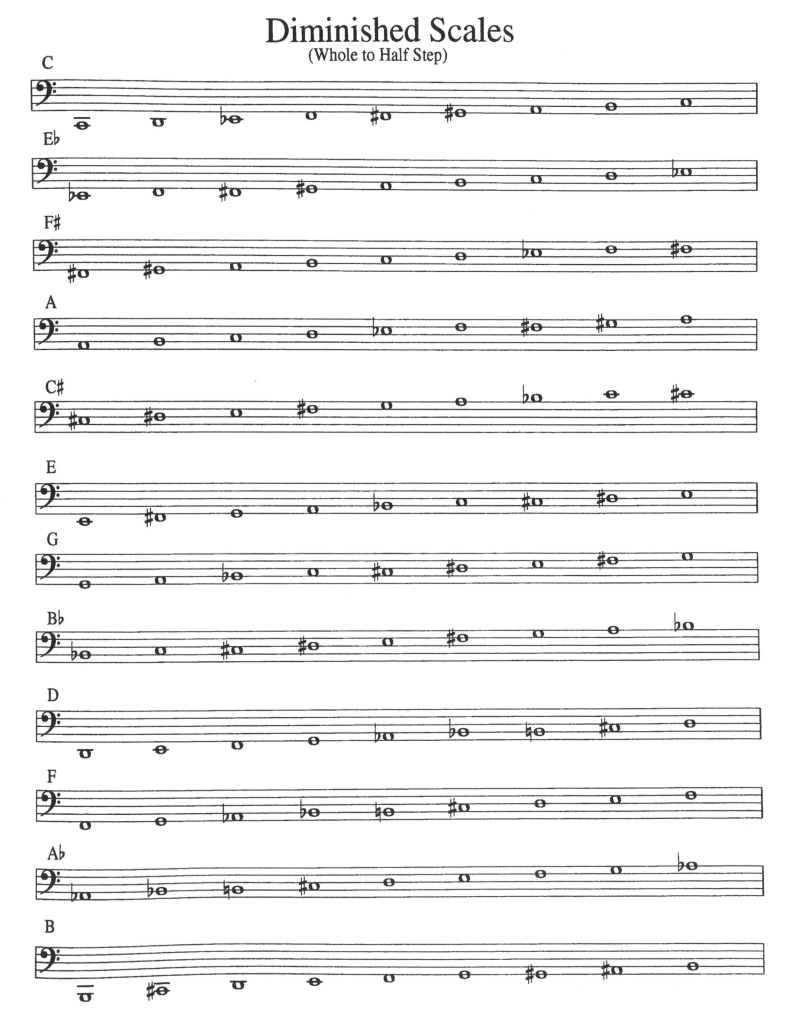

HALF-WHOLE STEP DIMINISHED SCALE

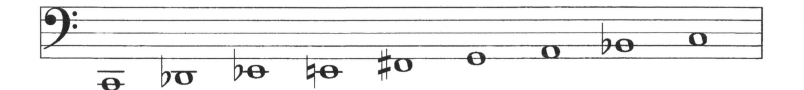

Half to Whole step diminished plays over;

1) Any dominant seven flat nine chord; i.e. C7b9=C half/whole step diminished

2) Any dominant seven sharp nine chord; i.e. C7#9=C half/whole step diminised

C Diminished Scale
(Half to Whole Step)

Ex.1 Horizontal

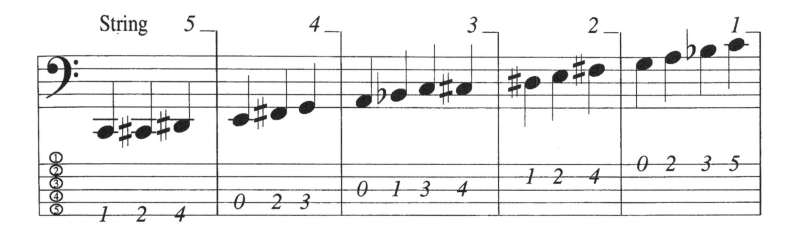

Ex. 2 Vertical

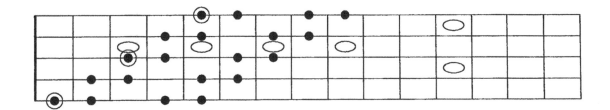

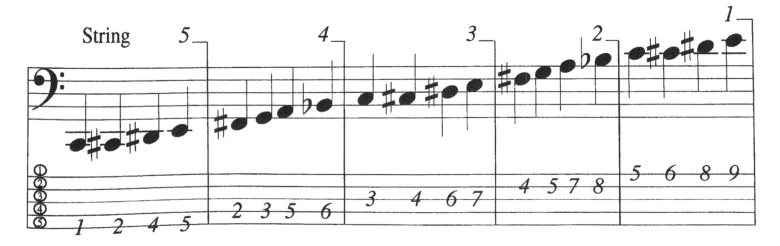

Diminished Scales
(Half to Whole Step)

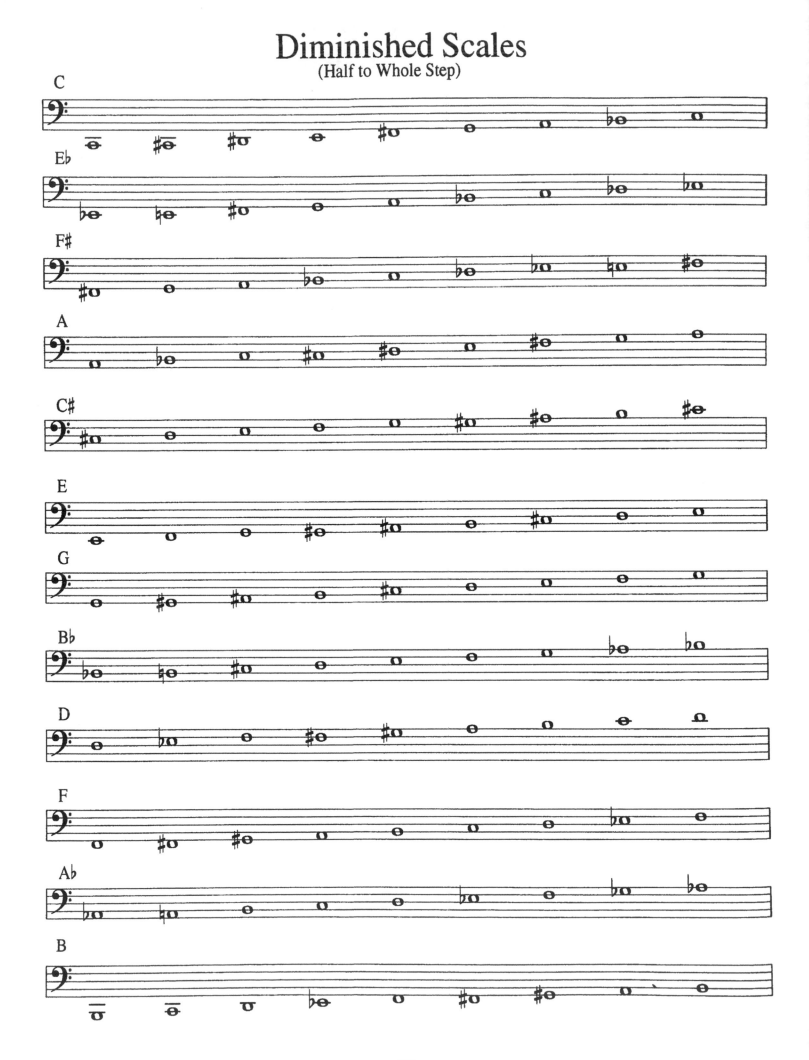

AUGMENTED SCALE

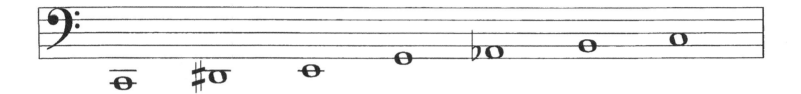

Augmented plays over;

1) Any major seven sharp five chord; i.e. C major7#5=C augmented

C Augmented Scale

Ex.1 Horizontal

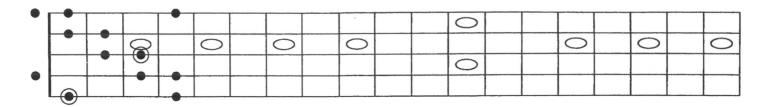

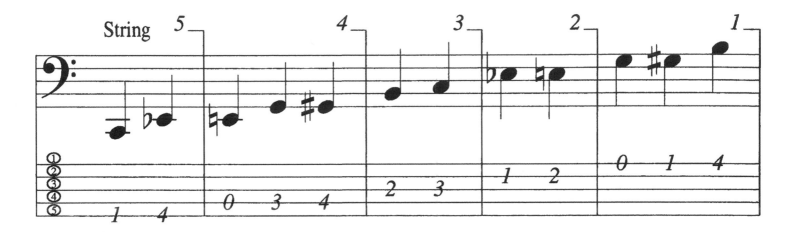

Ex. 2 Vertical

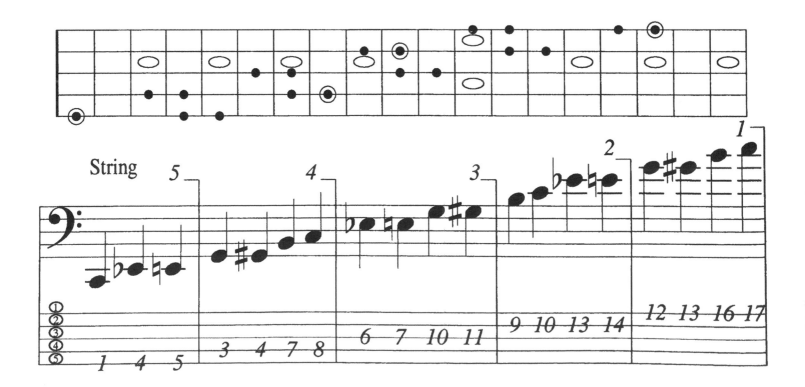

88

Augmented Scales

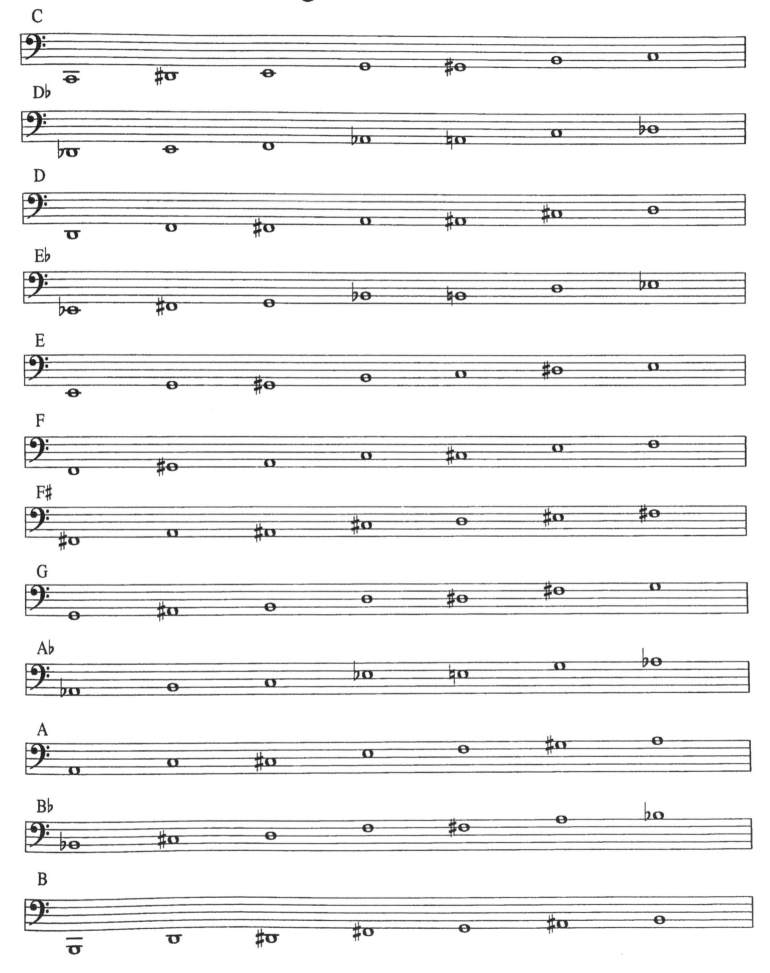

LYDIAN-AUGMENTED SCALE

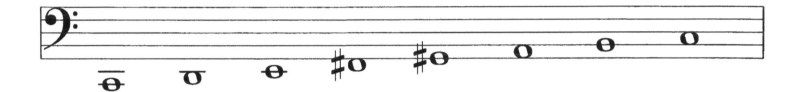

Lydian Augmented plays over;

1) Any Major sharp five chord; i.e. Cmajor7#5=C Lydian Augmented

C Lydian Augmented

Ex. 1 Horizontal

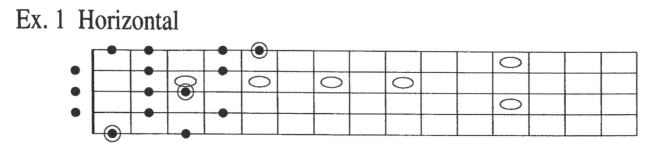

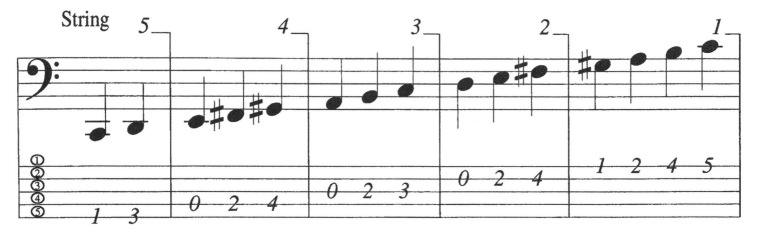

Ex. 2 Vertical

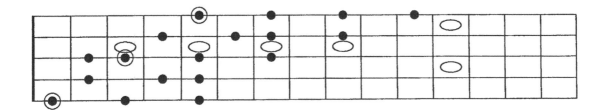

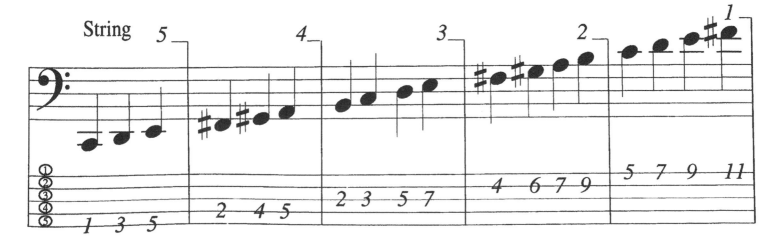

Lydian Augmented Scales

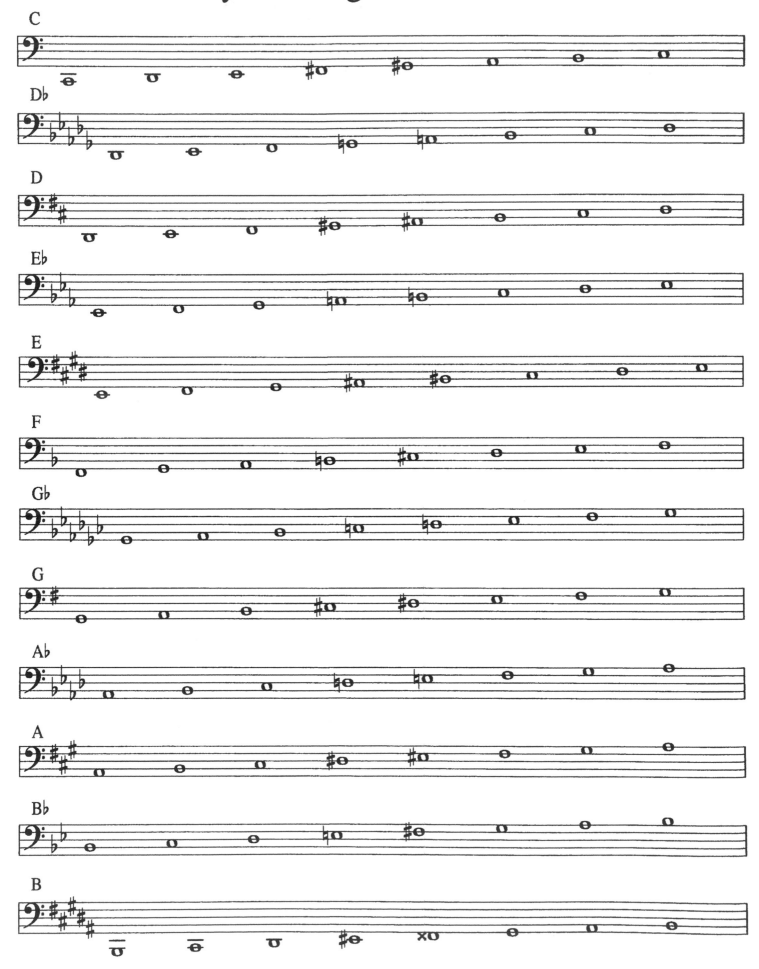

LYDIAN b7 SACLE

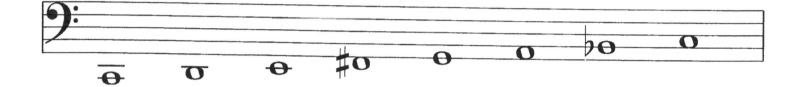

Lydian Flat Seven plays over;

1) Any dominant seven unaltered; i.e. C7=C Lydianb7

2) Any dominant seven flat five (#11); i.e. C7b5, C7#11=C Lydian b7

C Lydian b7 Scale

Ex. 1 Horizontal

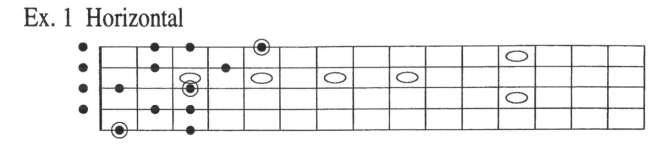

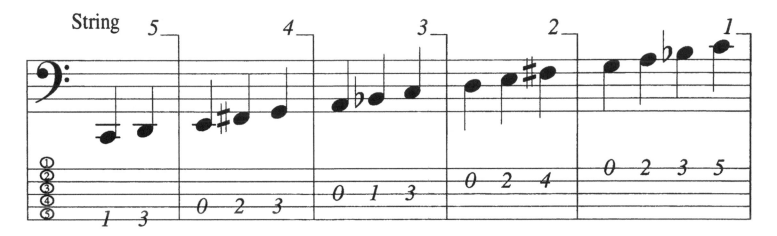

Ex. 2 Vertical

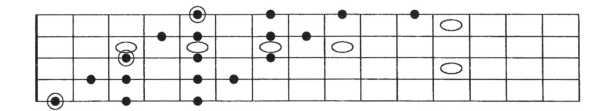

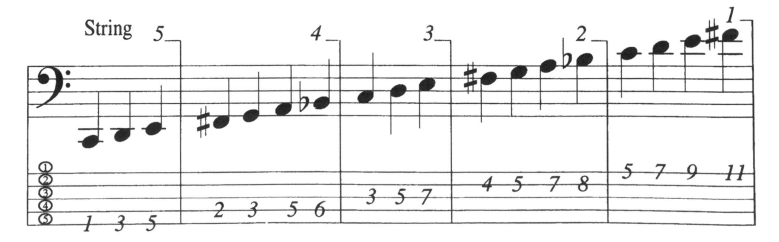

Lydian ♭7 Scales

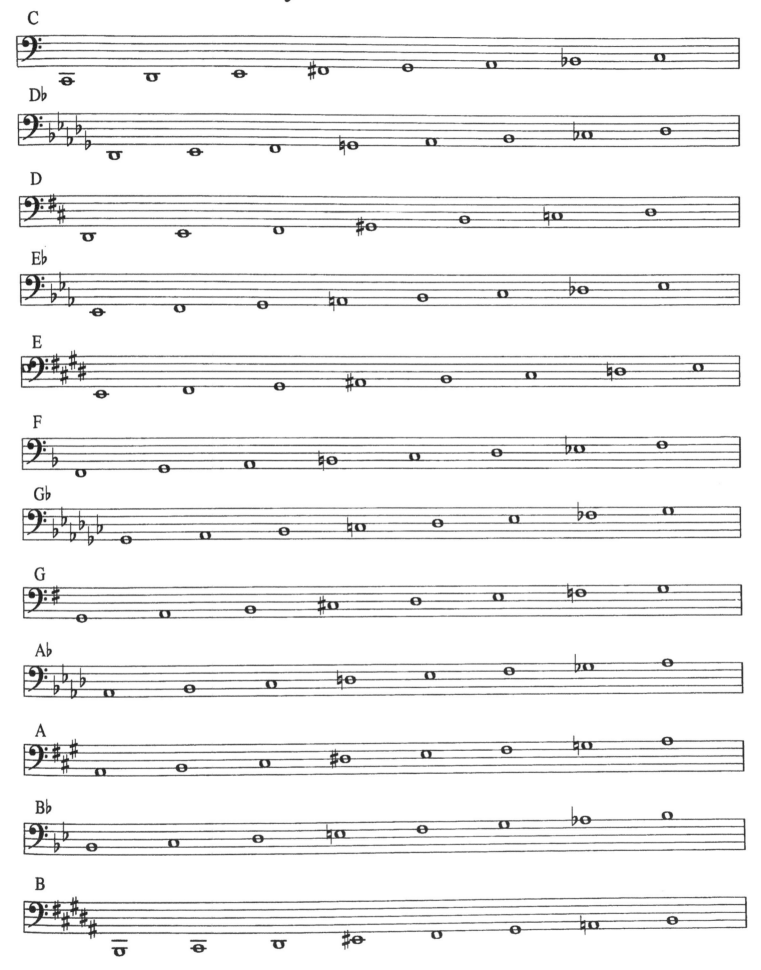

LOCRIAN #2 SCALE

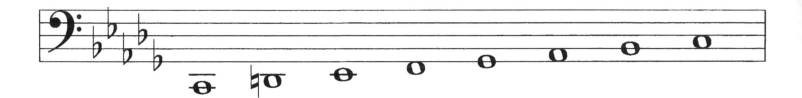

Locrian Sharp Two plays over;

1) Any half diminished chord; i.e. Cminor7b5=C locrian #2

2) Any minor nine flat five chord; i.e. Cminor9b5=C locrian#2

C Locrian #2 Scale

Ex. 1 Horizontal

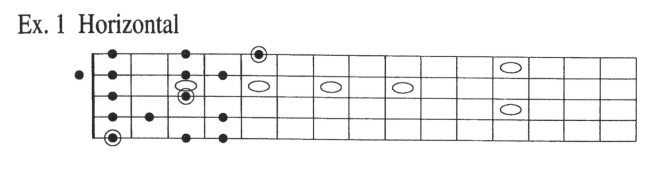

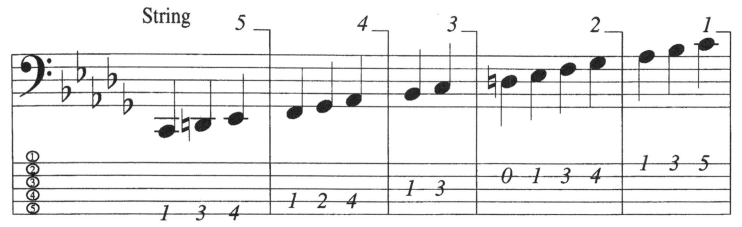

Ex. 2 Vertical

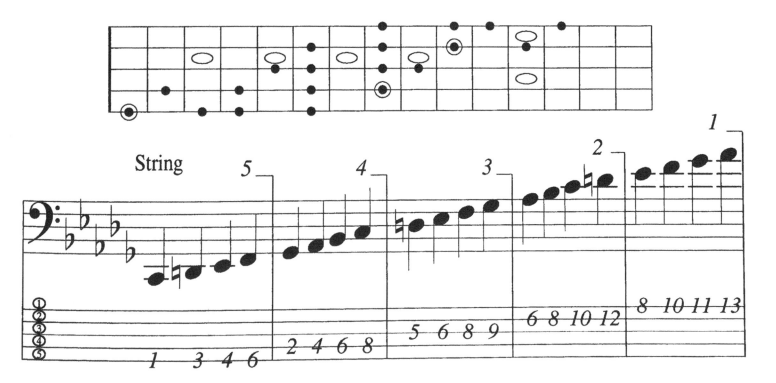

Locrian ♯2 Scales

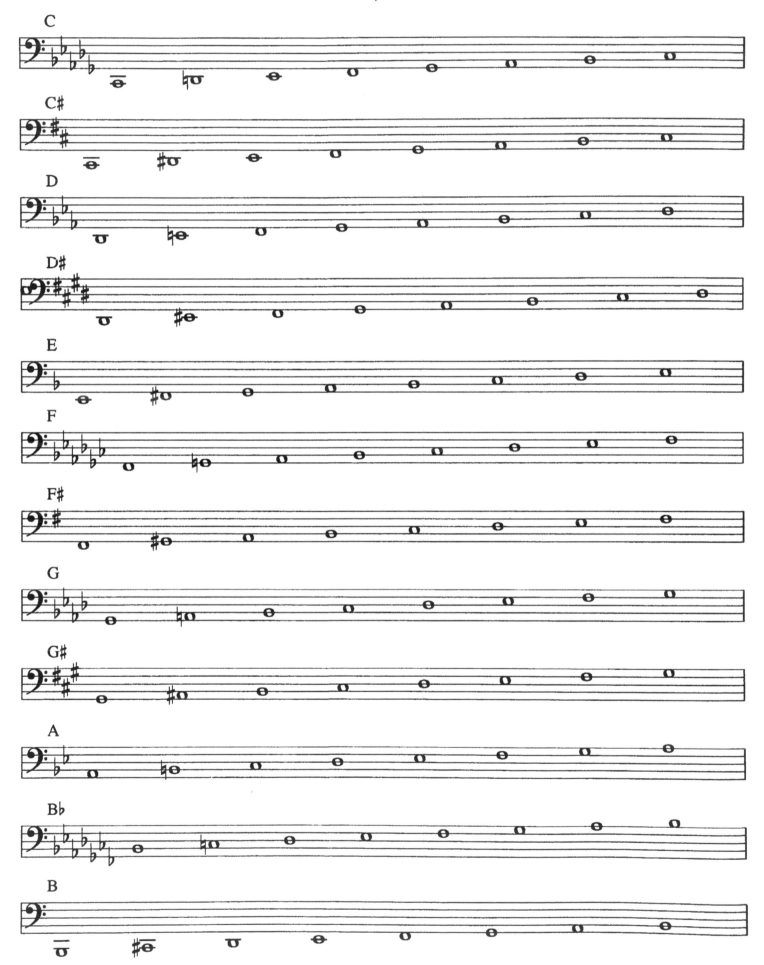

SUPER LOCRIAN SCALE

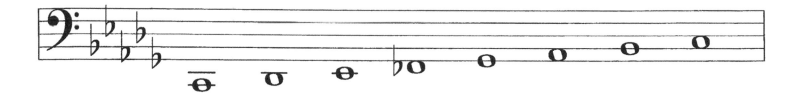

Super Locrian plays over;

1) Any dominant seven altered fifth or ninth; i.e. C7b5, C7#5, C7b9, C7#9, C7b5#9=C Super Locrian

C Super Locrian Scales

Ex. 1 Horizontal

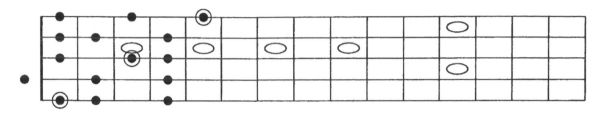

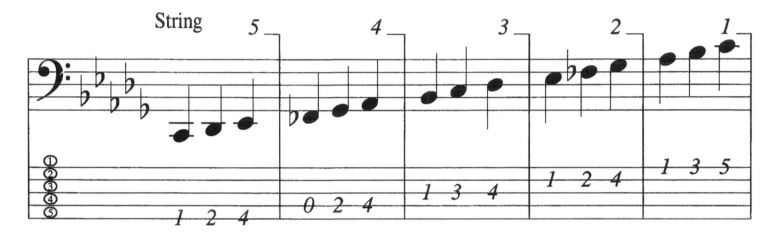

Ex. 2 Vertical

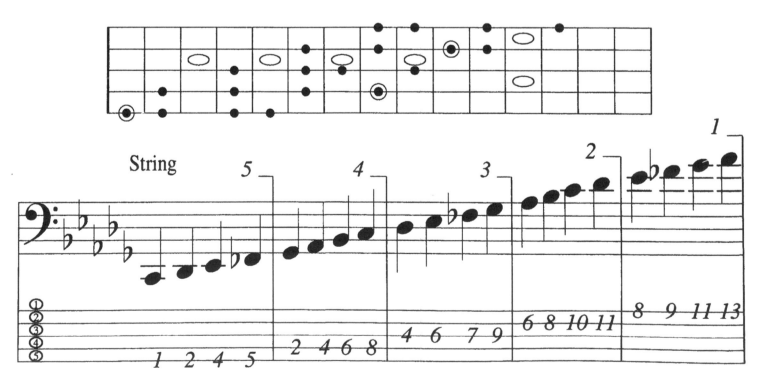

Super Locrian Scales

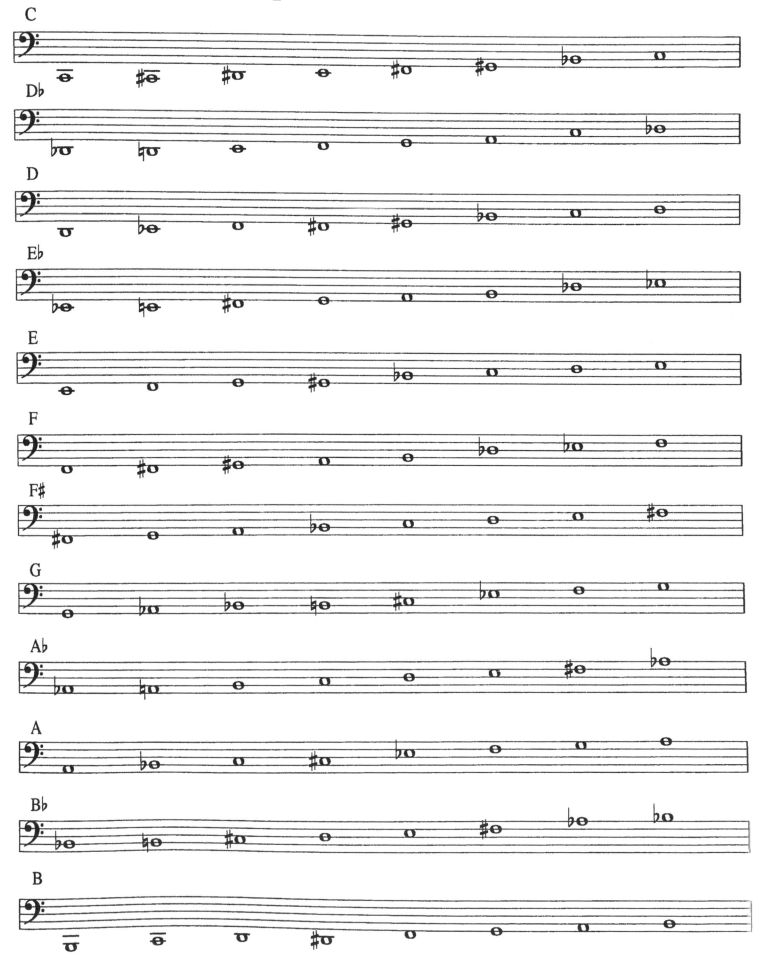

CHAPTER 3

5 STRING BASS GUITAR

FINGERBOARD CHART

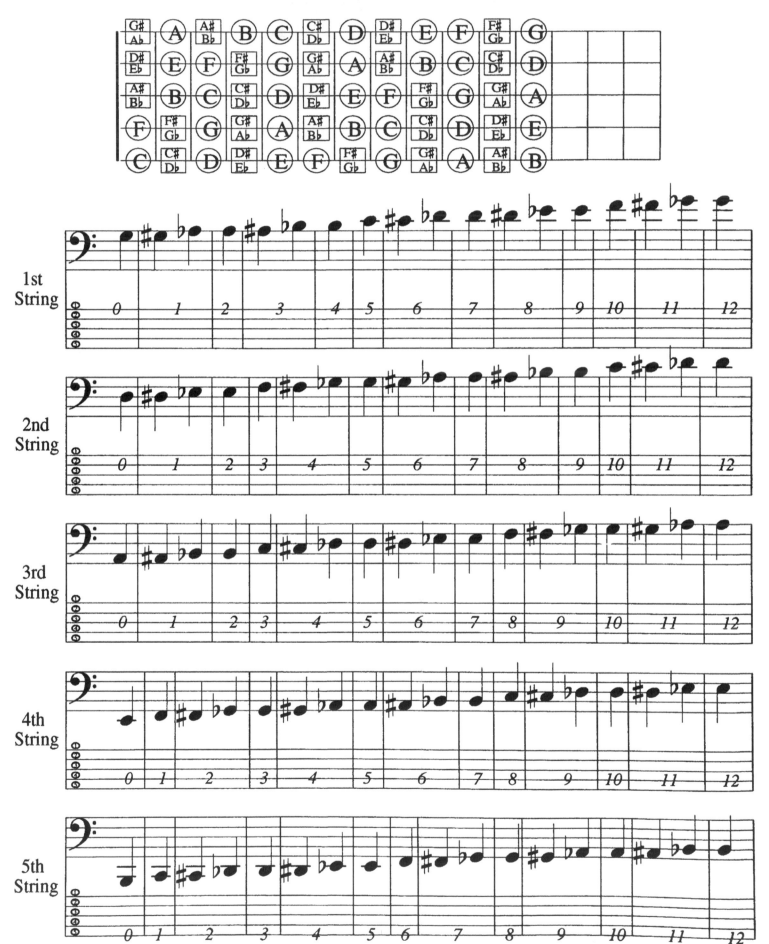

▼ = Root or Tonic

A,C#,E	A,C,E	A,C#,E,G	A,C,E,G
A	**A Minor**	**A 7**	**A Minor 7**

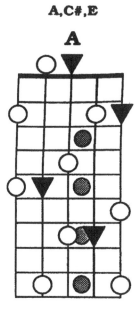 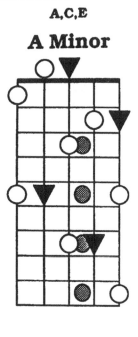 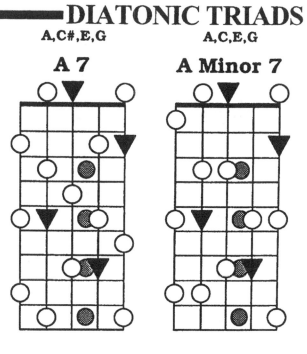 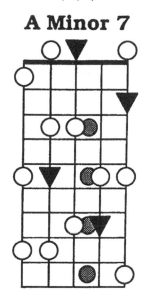

A,C#,E,F#	A,C,E,F#	A,C#,E,G#	A,C,E^b
A 6	**A Minor 6**	**A Major 7**	**A Dim.**

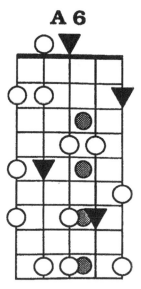 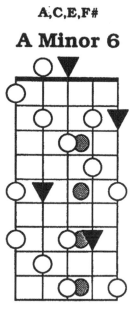 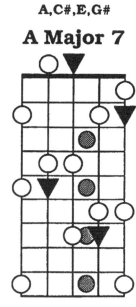

A,C#,E#	A,D,E,G
A Aug.	**A 7 Sus.**

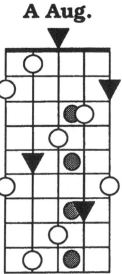 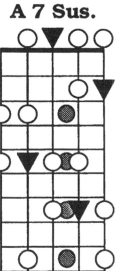

Bb-A#

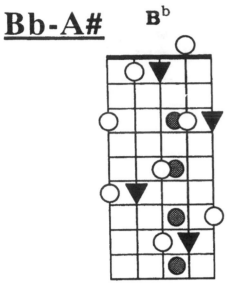

Bᵇ,D,F
Bᵇ
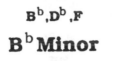

Bᵇ,Dᵇ,F
Bᵇ Minor
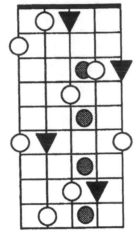

Bᵇ,D,F,Aᵇ
Bᵇ7
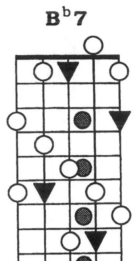

Bᵇ,Dᵇ,F,Aᵇ
Bᵇ Minor 7
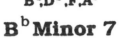
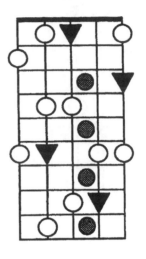

Bᵇ,D,F,E
Bᵇ6
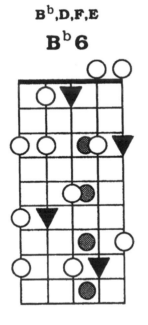

Bᵇ,Dᵇ,F,E
Bᵇ Minor 6
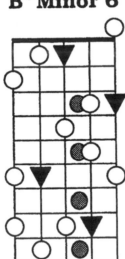

Bᵇ,D,F,♠
Bᵇ Major 7
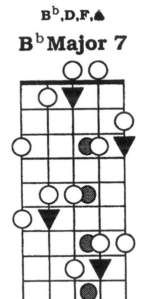

Bᵇ,Dᵇ,Fᵇ
Bᵇ Dim.
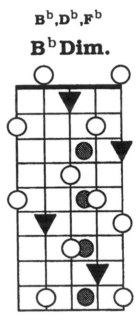

Bᵇ,D,F#
Bᵇ Aug.
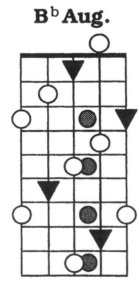

Bᵇ,Eᵇ,F,Aᵇ
Bᵇ7 Sus.
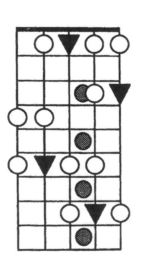

B,D#,F#
B

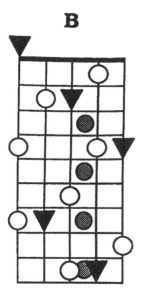

B,D,F#
B Minor

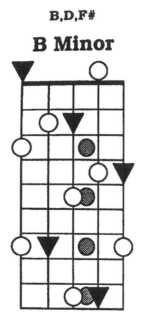

B,D#,F#,A
B 7

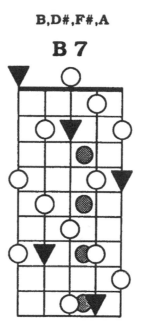

B,D,F#,A
B Minor 7

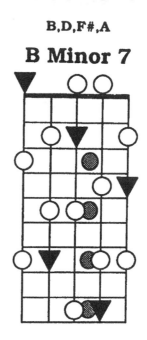

B,D#,F#,G#
B 6

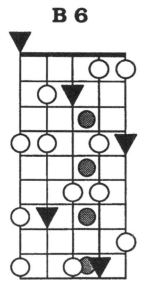

B,D,F#,G#
B Minor 6

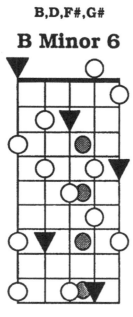

B,D#,F#,A#
B Major 7

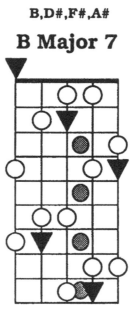

B,D,F
B Dim.

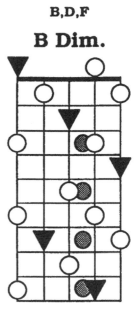

B,D#,F##
B Aug.

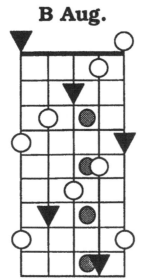

B,E,F#,A
B 7 Sus.

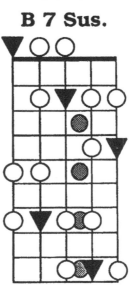

105

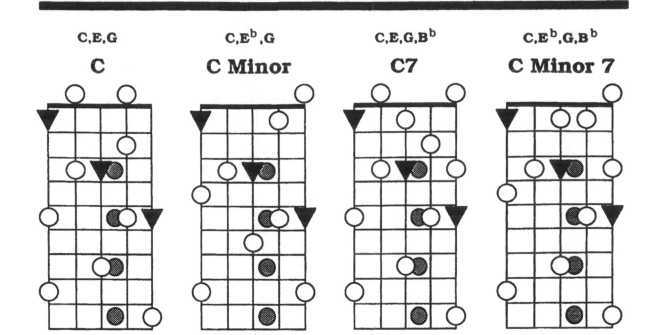

C
C,E,G

C Minor
C,E♭,G

C7
C,E,G,B♭

C Minor 7
C,E♭,G,B♭

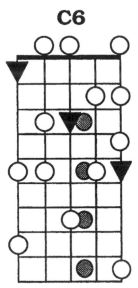

C6
C,E,G,A

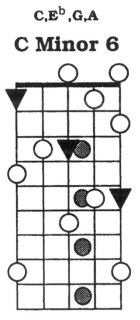

C Minor 6
C,E♭,G,A

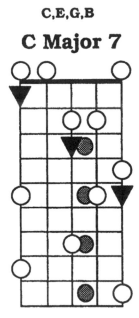

C Major 7
C,E,G,B

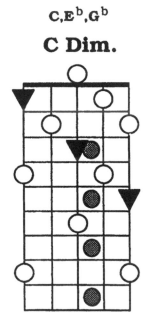

C Dim.
C,E♭,G♭

C Aug.
C,E,G#

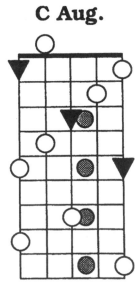

C 7 Sus.
C,F,G,B♭

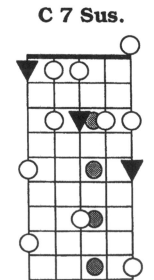

106

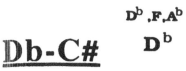

D^b ,F,A^b
D^b

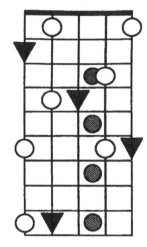

D^b ,F^b ,A^b
D^b Minor

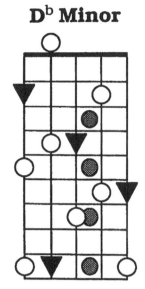

D^b ,F,A^b ,C^b
D^b 7

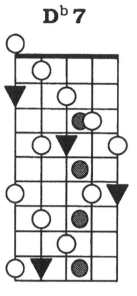

D^b ,F^b ,A^b ,C^b
D^b Minor 7

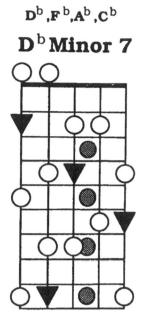

D^b ,F,A^b ,B^b
D^b 6

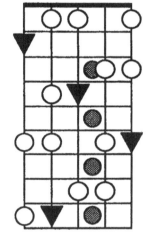

D^b ,F^b ,A^b ,B^b
D^b Minor 6

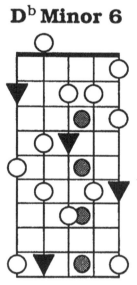

D^b ,F,A^b ,C
D^b Major 7

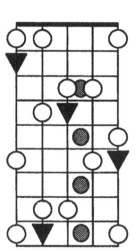
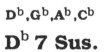

D^b ,F^b ,A^{bb}
D^b Dim.

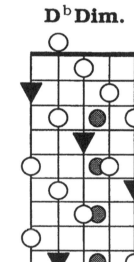

D^b ,F,A
D^b Aug.

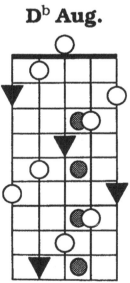

D^b ,G^b ,A^b ,C^b
D^b 7 Sus.

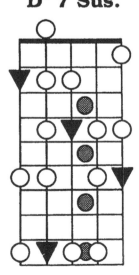

107

D,F#,A
D
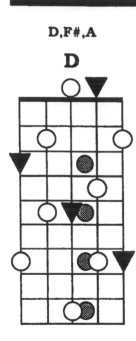

D,F,A
D Minor
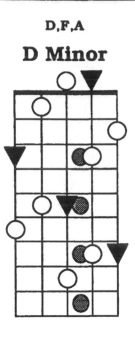

D,F#,A,C
D 7
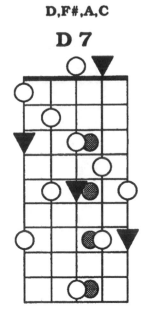

D,F,A,C
D Minor 7
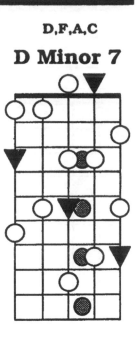

D,F#,A,B
D 6
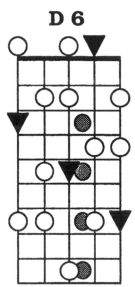

D,F,A,B
D Minor 6
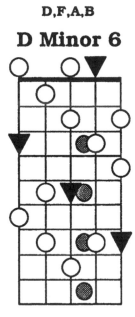

D,F#,A,C#
D Major 7

D,F,A^b
D Dim.
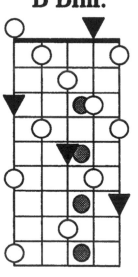

D,F#,A#
D Aug.
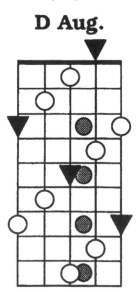

D,G,A,C
D 7 Sus.
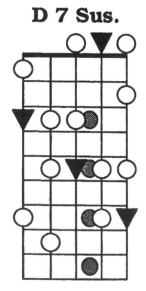

Eb-D#

E^b, G, B^b
E^b

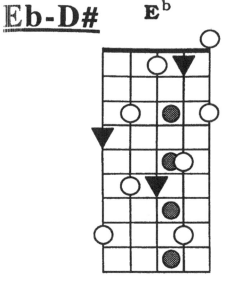

E^b, G^b, B^b
E^b Minor

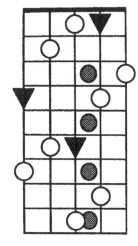

E^b, G, B^b, D^b
E^b 7

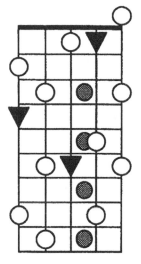

E^b, G^b, B^b, D^b
E^b Minor 7

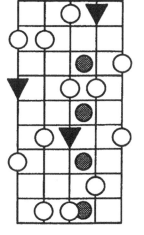

E^b, G, B^b, C
E^b 6

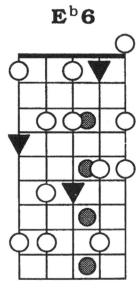

E^b, G^b, B^b, C
E^b Minor 6

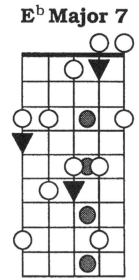

E^b, G, B^b, D
E^b Major 7

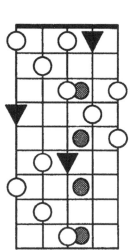

E^b, G^b, B^{bb}
E^b Dim.

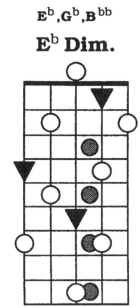

E^b, G, B
E^b Aug.

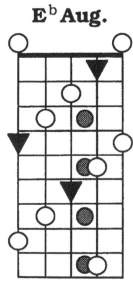

E^b, A^b, B^b, D^b
E^b 7 Sus.

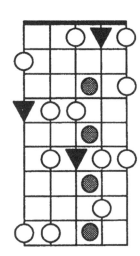

E,G#,B,
E
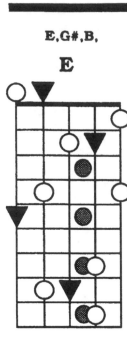

E,G,B
E Minor
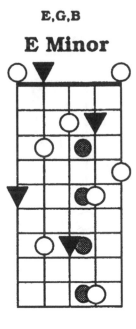

E,G#,B,D
E 7
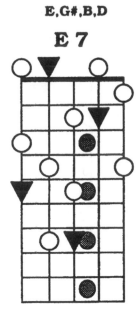

E,G,B,D
E Minor 7
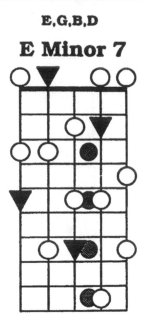

E,G#,B,C#
E 6
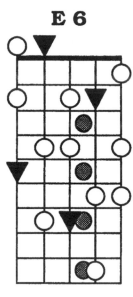

E,G,B,C#
E Minor 6
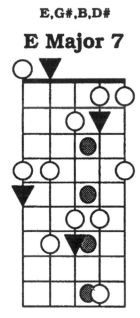

E,G#,B,D#
E Major 7

E,G,B^b
E Dim.
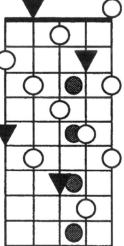

E,G,B#
E Aug.
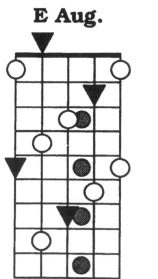

E,A,B,D
G 7 Sus.
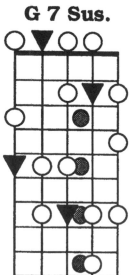

F
F,A,C

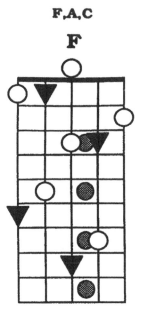

F Minor
F,A♭,C

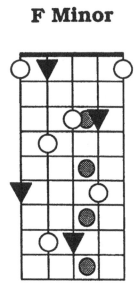

F 7
F,A,C,E♭

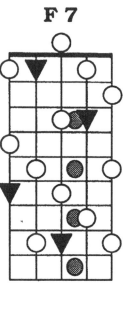

F Minor 7
F,A♭,C,E♭

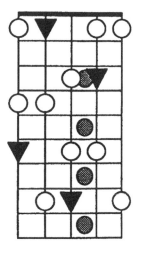

F 6
F,A,C,D

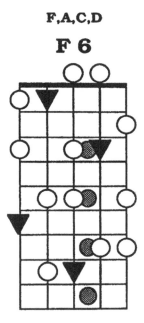

F Minor 6
F,A♭,C,D

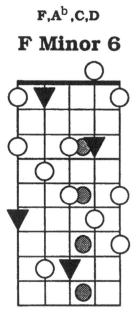

F Major 7
F,A,C,E

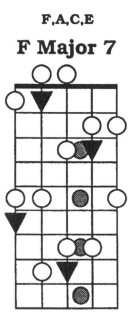

F Dim.
F,A♭,C♭

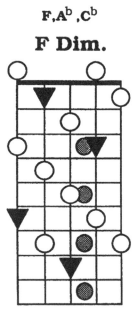

F Aug.
F,A,C#

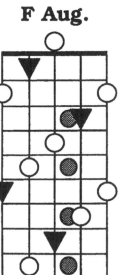

F 7 Sus.
F,B♭,C,E♭

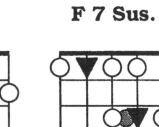
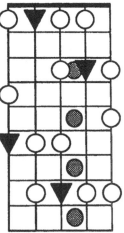

Gb-F#

Gb
Gb,Bb,Db

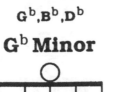

Gb Minor
Gb,Bb,Db

Gb 7
Gb,Bb,Db,Fb

Gb Minor 7
Gb,Bbb,Db,Fb

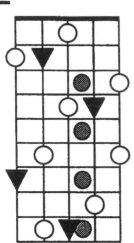
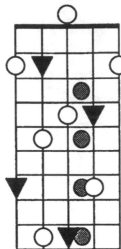
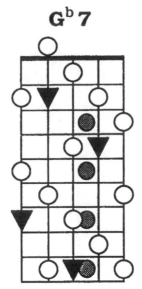
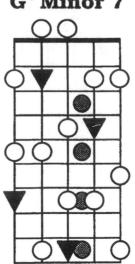

Gb 6
Gb,Bb,Db,Eb

Gb Minor 6
Gb,Bbb,Db,Eb

Gb Major 7
Gb,Bb,Db,F

Gb Dim.
Gb,Bbb,Dbb

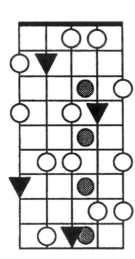
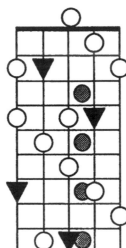
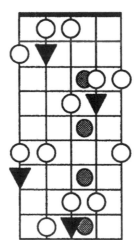
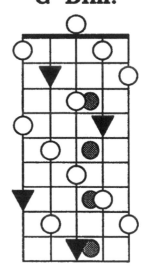

Gb Aug.
Gb,Bb,D

Gb 7 Sus.
Gb,Cb,Db,Fb

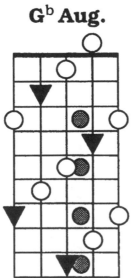
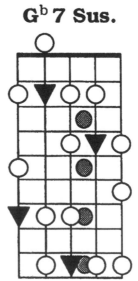

112

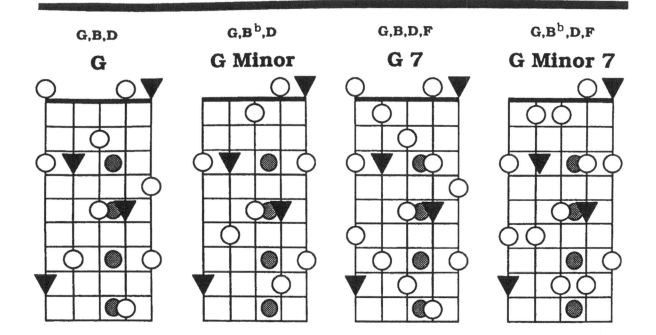

G
G,B,D

G Minor
G,B♭,D

G 7
G,B,D,F

G Minor 7
G,B♭,D,F

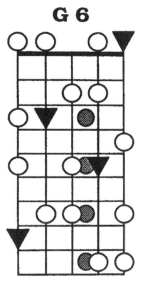 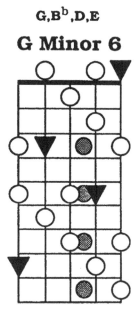 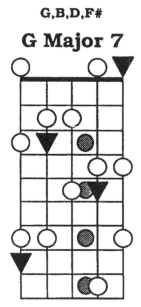 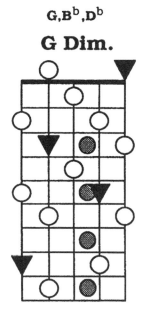

G 6
G,B,D,E

G Minor 6
G,B♭,D,E

G Major 7
G,B,D,F#

G Dim.
G,B♭,D♭

G Aug.
G,B,D#

G 7 Sus.
G,C,D,F

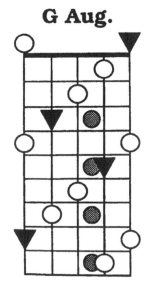 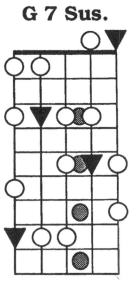

Ab-G#

A^b, C, E
A^b

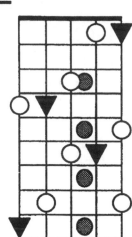

A^b, C^b, E^b
A^b Minor

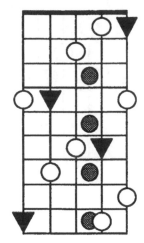

A^b, C, E^b, G^b
A^b 7

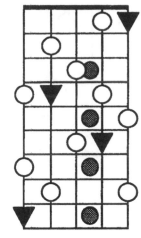

A^b, C^b, E^b, G^b
A^b Minor 7

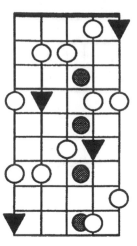

A^b, C, E^b, F
A^b 6

A^b, C^b, E^b, F
A^b Minor 6

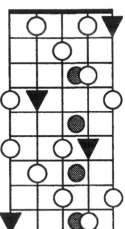

A^b, C, E^b, G
A^b Major 7

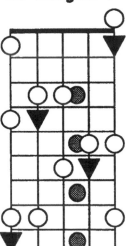

A^b, C^b, E^{bb}
A^b Dim.

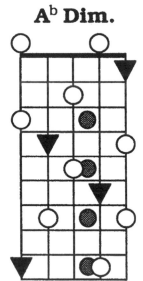

A^b, C, E
A^b Aug.

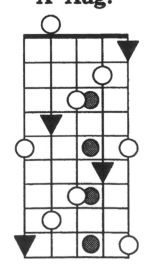

A^b, D^b, E^b, G^b
A^b 7 Sus.

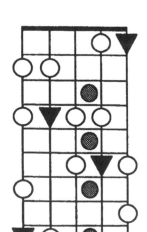

CHAPTER 4

Scale to chord guide

MAJOR CHORDS

Chord Type & Construction:	Scale Application:
1)Major 1, 3, 5	Major Pentatonic Minor Pentatonic on a 3rd Ionian
2) Major 7th 1, 3, 5, 7	Ionian Lydian Minor Pentatonic on the 7th Minor Pentatonic on a 3rd Harmonic Minor on a 3rd
3) Major 6th 1, 3, 5, 6	Major Pentatonic
4) Major 9th 1, 3, 5, 7, 9	Ionian Lydian
5) Major 6/9 1, 3, 5, 6, 9	Major Pentatonic Ionian
6) add 9 1, 3, 5, 9	Ionian Lydian Harmonic Minor on a 3rd
7) Major 7b5 1, 3, b5, 7	Lydian Minor Pentatonic on a 3rd
8) Major 7#5 1, 3, #5, 7	Lydian Augmented Augmented
9) Major 13 1, 3, 5, 7, 9, 13	Ionian Lydian
10) Suspended 4th 1, 4, 5	Ionian Minor Pentatonic on a 3rd
11) Major 7 #11 1, 3, 5, 7, 9, #11	Lydian

Scale to chord guide

Minor Chords

Chord Type & Construction:	Scale Application:
1) Minor 1, b3, 5	Minor Pentatonic Dorian Aeolian
2) Minor 7 1, b3, 5, b7	Dorian Aeolian Minor Pentatonic Blues Phrygian Harmonic Minor on a 5th

3) Minor 6 & 6/9
   1, b3, 5, 6
   1, b3, 5, 5, 9
	Dorian

4) Minor 7 Sus.4 1, b3, 4, b7	Dorian Minor Pentatonic Minor Pentatonic on a 5th
5) Minor #7 1, b3, 5, 7	Ascending Melodic Minor Harmonic Minor on a 5th
6) Minor 9 1, b3, 5, b7, 9	Minor Pentatonic Dorian Aeolian
7) Minor 11 1, b3, 5, b7, 9, 11	Minor Pentatonic Dorian Aeolian
8) Minor 13 1, b3, 5, b7, 9, 11, 13	Minor Pentatonic Dorian
9) Minor 7b5 1, b3, b5, b7	Locrian

Scale to chord guide

DOMINANT CHORDS

Chord Type & Construction:	Scale Application:
1) Dominant 7 1, 3, 5, b7	Mixolydian Lydian b7 Major Pentatonic
2) Dominant 7b5 or #11 1, 3, b5, b7, or 1, 3, b7, #11	Lydian b7
3) Dominant 7b5 or #5 1, 3, b5, (#5), b7	Whole Tone
4) Dominant 7#9 1, 3, 5, b7, #9	Half/Whole Step Diminished Dorian Blues Minor Pentatonic
5) Dominant 7b9 1, 3, 5, b7, b9	Half/Whole Step Diminished Harmonic Minor on a 4th
6) Dominant Altered 5th or 9th 1, 3, b5, b7 or 1, 3, 5, b7, #9 1, 3, #5, b7 or 1, 3, 5, b7, b9	Super Locrian Minor Pentatonic on a 3rd Major Pentatonic on 5th Whole Tone
7) Dominant 7 Sus.4 1, 4, 5, b7	Mixolydian Minor Pentatonic on the 2nd Minor Pentatonic on the 5th
8) Dominant 9 1, 3, 5, b7, 9	Mixolydian
9) Dominant 11 1, 3, 5, b7, 9, 11	Mixolydian
10) Dominant 13 1, 3, 5, b7, 9, 11, 13	Mixolydian

Scale to chord guide

HALF-DIMINISHED CHORDS

Chord Types & Construction:

Scale Application:

1) Half-Diminished
   1, b3, b5, b7

Locrian
Locrian #2
Harmonic Minor on the min.7th
Whole/Half Step Diminished

2) Minor 9b5
   1, b3, b5, b7, 9

Locrian #2

DIMINISHED CHORDS

1) Diminished 7
   1, b3, b5, b7

Whole/Half Step Diminished
Harmonic Minor on a min.2nd

AUGMENTED CHORDS

1) Augmented
   1, 3, #5

Whole Tone
Diminished/Whole Tone

BASS BOOKS FROM CENTERSTREAM

5-STRING BASS METHOD
by Brian Emmel
Besides discussing how to adapt to the differences in the 5-string versus 4-, this book explores the various ways of using the 5-string, practice tips, different techniques, and practical applications for various genres demonstrated through songs on the 37-minute accompanying CD.
00000134 Book/CD Pack $17.95

ART OF THE SLAP
by Brian Emmel
This slap bass method book, designed for advanced beginning to intermediate bassists, is based on the understanding and application of modes. The focus is on the concept of groove sculpting from modes, and not on actual right- and left-hand techniques. The CD features recordings of all the examples, plus a split-channel option to let you practice your playing. Includes 13 songs.
00000229 Book/CD Pack..$16.95

BASS GUITAR CHORDS
by Ron Middlebrook
84 of the most popular chords for bass guitar. Covers: finger placement, note construction, chromatic charts, and the most commonly used bass scales. Also has a helpful explanation of the common 2-5-1 progression, and the chords in all keys.
00000073 ....$2.95

BEGINNING TO ADVANCED 4-STRING BASS
DVD
by Brian Emmel
This instructional video by noted instructor/author Brian Emmel leaves no stone unturned in explaining all there is to know about 4-string bass basics! Designed for the beginning to advanced player, Brian's step-by-step demonstrations form the foundation for understanding music theory and building bass technique. Topics covered range from common musical terminology, to playing in a garage band, to laying down tracks in a recording studio. 60 minutes.
00000374 DVD $19.95

BLUES GROOVES
Traditional Concepts for Playing 4 & 5 String Blues Bass
by Brian Emmel
This book/CD pack has been designed to educate bass enthusiasts about the development of different styles and traditions throughout the history of the blues, from the 1920s to the early 1970s. Players will learn blues scales, rhythm variations, turnarounds, endings and grooves, and styles such as Chicago blues, jazz, Texas blues, rockabilly, R&B and more. The CD includes 36 helpful example tracks.
00000269 Book/CD Pack $17.95

PURRFECT 4-STRING BASS METHOD
by Brian Emmel
This book will teach students how to sight read and to acquire a musical vocabulary. Includes progressive exercises on rhythm notation, 1st to 4th string studies, enharmonic studies, chords and arpeggios, blues progressions, and chord charts.
00000201 ....$9.95

New

ULTIMATE BASS EXERCISES
Bassist and educator Max Palermo takes you through more than 700 easy, step-by-step exercises for finger building, based on the 24 possible fingering combinations. 158 pages.
00000476 ....$19.95

CENTERSTREAM

Email: Centerstrm@aol.com
Phone (714) 779-9390